Yen-Rong Wong is an arts critic and award-winning writer working between Yugambeh and Jagera and Turrbal lands. She won the Glendower Award for an Emerging Queensland Writer in 2022, and the Queensland Premier's Young Publishers and Writers Award in 2020. She has been a Wheeler Centre Hot Desk fellow and writer-in-residence at the Katharine Susannah Prichard Writers' Centre. She is a frequent contributor to *The Saturday Paper* as a theatre critic, and her work has appeared in many print and online publications, including *The Guardian*, *Sydney Review of Books*, *Meanjin*, and *Griffith Review*. *Me, Her, Us* is her debut book of non-fiction.

First published 2023 by University of Queensland Press
PO Box 6042, St Lucia, Queensland 4067 Australia

University of Queensland Press (UQP) acknowledges the Traditional Owners and their
custodianship of the lands on which UQP operates. We pay our respects to their Ancestors and
their descendants, who continue cultural and spiritual connections to Country. We recognise
their valuable contributions to Australian and global society.

uqp.com.au
reception@uqp.com.au

Cover design by Jenna Lee
Author photograph by Declan Roache
Typeset in 12.5/17.5 pt Adobe Garamond Pro by Post Pre-press Group, Brisbane
Printed in Australia by McPherson's Printing Group

This manuscript won the 2022 Glendower Award for an Emerging Queensland Writer, which
is generously supported by Jenny Summerson. UQP launched the Emerging Queensland
Writer Award in 1999. Presented as part of the Queensland Literary Awards, in partnership
with State Library of Queensland, UQP is proud to publish the annual award-winning
manuscript, and is committed to building the profile of, and access to, emerging writers in
Australia and internationally.

UQP is assisted by the Australian Government through
the Australia Council, its arts funding and advisory
body.

A catalogue record for this book is available from the National Library of Australia

ISBN 978 0 7022 6620 1 (pbk)
ISBN 978 0 7022 6800 7 (epdf)
ISBN 978 0 7022 6801 4 (epub)

This started out as a letter to my younger self, but it's really for all young Asian women. It's for those of you who feel stifled by familial expectation, those of you who feel like you have to make a choice between the cultures you belong to and participate in. It's for young women who look different, for women who have 'foreign-looking' names, for those who have complicated relationships with their parents.

I want you to know: you are not alone.

Contents

Author's Note

It is upsetting and shocking (though not surprising) that very little work about sex and relationships from the perspective of an Asian* Australian woman has been published in Australia. Discourse around sex in this country is typically framed through a white (and often male) lens, resulting in a flattening of experiences and disengagement from young people of colour. Though progress has been made in regard to queer and trans experiences, there is still hesitancy when it comes to doing the

---

* I acknowledge the false homogeneity of the term 'Asian', but in many instances it is the best word to use for the purposes of brevity and for this collection. I also acknowledge my light-skinned privilege, and that in some instances, in some societies, it is a privilege afforded to me because of my Chinese background and my Chinese features. I choose to use the term 'Chinese-presenting' because flattening of the Chinese diaspora, especially in Western countries, means I am often tagged as Chinese – that is, from China – when the reality of my ethnic identity is more complicated and nuanced than this one word.

same with regard to race. Representations of sex in media are also either unrealistic or centre trauma, leaving little space for deeper and more complex conversations.

This book aims to remedy this gap. It is split into three sections: 'Me' focuses solely on my experiences of sex as it relates to shame, pleasure, and kink, before moving on to 'Her', which provides a deeper insight into my childhood, my relationship with my mother, and the ways in which these experiences have moulded my attitudes towards sex. Finally, 'Us' explores the roles that fetishisation, white supremacy, and Orientalism play in the Asian diaspora, especially as they pertain to sex, relationships, and desire.

Most of the relationships I have written about are relationships with men, because I've considered myself straight for much of my life to date. I realised about halfway through writing this book that I'd harboured an incorrect conception of bisexuality for the majority of my adult life, and that it was time to embrace and accept my bisexuality and queerness. In recent years, I've also been introduced to the world of polyamory, ethical non-monogamy, and relationship anarchy: new ways of framing relationships – whether they be romantic, platonic, collegial, or otherwise. I don't talk about these much in this book because I am still new to these circles. I haven't had enough time to properly digest these new identities, what they mean in relation to my upbringing, and the way I see myself in the future. I would be doing a disservice to myself and these communities at large if I were to discuss them without properly interrogating my relationship to these labels.

However, this book is still representative of the work I wish I could have read when I was a young adult, if only to feel a little less alone and lost while trying to figure my way through the world. It is my sincere hope that it might be able to do so for other young women.

1

Shame

I am naked, lying in his bed under a pale-blue waffle-weave blanket. The rumpled cream sheets are soft against my bare skin, and my eyes are glued to the ceiling. The only light in the room comes through the slightly drawn curtains on the window to my right.

I'm struggling – not physically, not outwardly – but there is a knot in my stomach. It makes me feel like a stone statue nestled in a bed of cotton wool. The knot is immobilising. It is a dense, compact furball of emotion that I can't cough up, a weight that means I can't move without a feeling of dread sinking ever deeper into my stomach. It feels like days of period cramps combined with the first days of a full-blown depressive episode, concentrated into one small area near my belly button. It feels like a psychological manifestation of an autoimmune response; it is a knot that tells me I've done something very, very wrong.

It goes away, eventually. But it's a slow process, and while it lingers, all I can do is wait for it to dissipate. It is not the first time this has happened, and not the first time in this bed.

It has been there since I was young – growing, calcifying, fortifying itself with age. It feeds off old adages, rules, anxieties, wanting and needing to be a good girl – a good *Chinese* girl – a good daughter, a good girlfriend. I haven't told him about this, because I'm afraid he won't understand. This is my first long-term relationship, and I'm afraid it might scare him away. I also don't want to give anyone else any more of myself than I have to, and the risk here does not seem worth the potential reward.

I hear the faint sounds of the shower through two rooms' worth of walls – he's gone to the bathroom to clean himself up. He's left me to recover, saving me from trying to explain why I'm frozen in place. Usually, by the time he's back, his mousy-brown hair slightly damp and a towel wrapped loosely around his waist, I'm all right. If not, it's easy enough to make up an excuse so I can continue to lie prone on the bed, hurting but not really hurting, waiting for this strange, ugly feeling to pass.

It's not his fault. It's not my fault, either, but I don't really believe that yet. I convince myself that I must be doing something wrong; after all, it is my body that is reacting like this – he seems to be completely fine. I feel like I am doing sex wrong, whatever that means. Or, at least, I'm not doing it *right*. How else is it that one minute I am gasping with pleasure, endorphins running through my veins – and the next, my body feels like it will collapse in on itself if I move? Maybe it's something unique to me that will never go away, something I will just have to deal with every time I have sex. I have no other way to explain how the knot sinks into my stomach and sticks there, how it makes me feel like a failure, like I am not worthy of sex, of love, of pleasure.

I grew up in a small family – just me, my parents, and my younger sister. We lived in the depths of Brisbane's southern suburbs, surrounded by bushland that has since been cut down and developed into rows of cookie-cutter townhouses. When I was five, we moved into a two-storey brick house with a pool and a cubbyhouse in the backyard, and my parents have lived there ever since.

Whenever I go home, a dark-brown bevelled wooden cross stares at me from across the dining-room table. It has been there for nearly twenty years, a constant figure in my life. Our family started attending a particular church after my sister was born in 1996, and the cross was the congregation's gift to my parents when we first moved into the house – a symbol of our (their) faith, a symbol of protection. I remember the day it arrived, accompanied by the chatter of Taiwanese aunties and uncles. My sister and I were playing in the corner of the rumpus room we'd made into a 'secret playroom' when Mum came to show it to us. '好漂亮哦,' she gushed.

This light piece of wood holds an oppressive weight. It holds within it years of obedience, pain, and control. It is always the first thing that catches my eye when I go home; I see it from the moment I step onto the cold tiled floor. It is a reminder that my parents still think I believe in their God – that I *should* still believe in their God.

My family's identity as Chinese Christians has shadowed my dating life. I was supposed to find a nice, Christian, Chinese boy – preferably from our church, but it would be okay as long as he went to *a* church of some kind. Dating (or, even worse, marrying) someone who didn't fit this description would be a mark against me and, more importantly, my family. I know I'm not alone in this experience, and I'm reminded of it every time I introduce a friend to *Kim's Convenience* (CBC Television, 2016–2021). The pilot episode of this series features Umma urging her adult daughter, Janet, to date a 'cool, Christian, Korean boy', even going so far as to set her up without her knowledge, believing this to be the only viable choice.

I was raised to believe in the purity of the nuclear family, that the correct – read: natural – life progression involved school, university, a well-paying job, a good Chinese boy, marriage, a house, children, and, in general, a fairytale-esque happily ever after. I 'dated' in high school, but nothing serious – my longest relationship only lasted a couple of months. I was too busy studying, and probably too immature for anything to last. My parents' expectations regarding my relationships were all unspoken, of course – they emanated strongly enough off that wooden cross to prevent my sister or me from daring to challenge our parents or their beliefs. These rules also governed the way we dressed, how we should behave, and, sometimes, even when to speak. It was assumed that we'd do as we were expected, without complaint or question.

My parents also didn't actively encourage my sister or me to talk about our emotions. I'm not even sure if they talked to each other about their emotions. Everything – good and bad – was suppressed. It was almost as if the image we had to project to the outside world had at some point stopped becoming a performance and just became the way we lived. I don't think I realised how much energy this took out of me until I started living alone, how, for the first time ever, I knew what it was to feel relaxed – or, at least, a little more relaxed than I had felt for the past twenty years of my life.

I'm more honest with myself these days, because I know the harm I'm doing to myself if I'm not. I allow myself to be sad, frustrated, jealous, happy. The walls snap back up when I'm with my parents, though. It's an instinct, a survival mechanism, the only way I know how to be as authentic as I can be without exposing myself to further scrutiny or criticism. As much as I hate to admit it, I know that as a Chinese daughter my life is not just my own; I am an unavoidable point of consideration when it comes to my parents' standing in their communities. So when I'm home, the least I can do is not to say or do anything in front of them that would make them ashamed of me.

I remember a conversation in Dad's old, nearly run-down, white Toyota Camry – I was about six or seven. We were stopped at the set of traffic lights just before the school parking lot. I was sitting in the front seat, and I had been thinking.

'如果我長大的時候找不到男朋友, 那怎麼樣呢?' I asked Dad. I was genuinely concerned.

'沒關係,' he responded, smiling. '上帝會好好照顧你.'

His answer satisfied me. I trusted him. I trusted God. I didn't know any better. We didn't talk about anything related to sex or marriage again until I was twenty.

I lost my virginity in a one-bedroom apartment in the Brisbane CBD.

I lost my virginity to a boy from school, who later turned out to be an arsehole. I was surprised that I enjoyed it, in spite of our collective clumsiness and inexperience.

I fucked him again – the first boy of many. I figured out what boys usually liked, how they liked it, what things to say, how to move my body and my mouth, when to go for it, and when to back off. More importantly, I figured out what I liked: someone to pull my hair, to bite me, to fuck me hard and fast while whispering obscenities into my ear, but also someone who would stroke my hair afterwards and trace their fingers down my spine and kiss me on the forehead when I woke up. It was bittersweet, because the more sex I had, the more I wanted – almost needed – it. I wanted that rush of endorphins, that feeling of power – and, occasionally, that feeling of powerlessness. I felt guilty for wanting sex, for wanting more of it even after those boys were done and I was done. I felt greedy, like I'd been allowed to run amok in a bookstore without adult supervision.

And even though I wanted to have as much sex as I could with as many people as I could to rip the pages out of this rulebook I had internalised, there was always that voice in the back of my mind, asking, *What would Mum and Dad think if they knew what you were doing right now?*

I met G at my first 'proper' party – that is, one with alcohol – when I was seventeen. It was a rare moment of teenage freedom; I was only allowed to go because it was a quick two-minute drive from my parents' house (at this point in time, I hadn't been to a party since I was in year two), and one of my friends promised to have me home before ten.

We chatted and drank and a friend dared me to make out with him. I'm surprised I didn't fall over as I drunkenly approached and propositioned him, and I'm even more surprised that our relationship developed over the summer of 2012. We talked about mental health, our families, and our fucked-up childhoods. We talked about how hard it can be to navigate all this, and it was nice to have someone who understood, even if I didn't really know how or why. He tried to get me to try weed, especially after I found his fancy glass bong in the back of his wardrobe. I didn't and still don't do drugs, because I don't want my brain chemistry to be any more fucked up than it is already. I told him this, but added that I had no problem with him getting high when I was around. He continued to push anyway. Nearly thirty-year-old me is impressed by eighteen-year-old me's tenacity in the face of overwhelming pressure.

We sexted often. We sexted while I was in bed and he was hiding under an old Queenslander during a drunk game of hide-and-seek. We sexted while he was in bed and I was practising hymn accompaniments on the grand piano at church. My sister once picked up my phone by accident, read one of his replies, and reacted by tossing it to me, screaming 'EW!', and scrunching her face up as tightly as possible. I was embarrassed, but I didn't stop sexting. He laughed when I recounted this story later, and he laughed at the fact I still went to church.

During this time, despite a lifetime of going to church with my deeply religious parents, I found myself losing my faith. God had not provided for me; prayer (on my parents' advice) had not saved me from endless bullying, depression, and thoughts of suicide. I went through the motions at church, and I felt guilty for pretending to be as enthusiastic as everyone else there. I was afraid I would be caught out, but at the time more attention was being paid to recruiting young university students from Taiwan and China to the church than keeping those who had supposedly been indoctrinated. I didn't tell my parents. I didn't want to deal with the anger and the guilt-tripping that would most definitely be inflicted on me if I came clean.

I went to house parties, I drank, I met boys. I found out I was, in fact, attractive. I tried the casual sex thing for a bit even though I wasn't in the right headspace to be sleeping around. Sometimes I felt guilty for not being in a relationship, for willingly giving myself to someone without getting anything in return. Sometimes I felt guilty for lying to my parents about where I was because I was busy fucking G, who at the time lived in a five-person sharehouse in St Lucia. The knot was there, sometimes, and I might have felt it if I wasn't so busy trying to cram so much into my newly found freedom. If I'd slowed down to think about what I was doing, I might have figured out that something was wrong, but the hormone soup in my brain hadn't yet stabilised, and I was too stressed about balancing twenty-something contact hours at uni with work and too worried about making my 9.00 pm curfew to notice.

Maybe it was the knot that led me to second-guess myself when it came to G. I wondered if I was being too needy or clingy and if I needed to pull back. Absence makes the heart grow fonder, or some kind of bullshit like that. I tried not to text as much or as often. I tried to remember what the rule was on texting after dates, but I couldn't find any sort of consensus among my friends, or on the internet.

We were never officially 'dating', and in any case all my attempts to be more aloof didn't work. After a few weeks of mismatched schedules, we arranged to meet one Wednesday evening. I'd just finished work, and he was home after a meeting at university.

The carpet in the hallway crunched softly as I walked to his room.

'Hey.'

He was sitting in his chair, facing his computer. He turned around, briefly meeting my eyes. I could tell his attention was still mostly on the computer screen.

'I don't think this is working out,' he told me.

I didn't know what to say, so I didn't say anything. The carpet felt scratchier under my feet, pricking me through my socks. My mind was racing through escape routes, ways to get out of the conversation, ways to get out of the room and the house without attracting attention to myself. Tears welled up in my eyes, and I forced myself to blink them away.

I waited. Normally, I would have dug in my heels and fought; I would have come up with some sort of reason why I thought he was wrong. But this time, against my basest judgements, I waited.

'I don't think you're as attractive as I thought you were,' he said. A new game of *DotA* flashed up on his computer screen, and I walked out of his room and out of the house. I hurt, but in a new way. It felt almost like a betrayal. I was ashamed to admit to myself that I was ever attracted to him.

The character for sin in Chinese is 罪. Even now, the sight of the character makes me cringe, and hearing it spoken aloud makes me think of blood and shame and guilt. No-one ever explained to me *why* it was a sin to have sex before marriage, but I was raised to be a good girl, to listen to and obey my parents and the church, so I didn't question it. Upon reflection, it makes sense, in a twisted kind of way. After all, if you believe God has prepared the perfect man or woman for you, why would you need to go and find other people to sleep with? It's almost accusatory – who are you to think you know better than

God? Why isn't your trust and faith in God strong enough to overcome temptations of the flesh?

Even though I was having fun exploring my new-found freedom, I still went to church every Sunday, in my Sunday best, with my family none the wiser. I knew the rituals of a Sunday congregation off by heart, so it was easy for me to pretend I still believed, that I was still a good Christian girl. There were two designated times for prayer during the service, and I knew I probably should have been asking for some kind of forgiveness for all the sex I'd been having and all the lying I'd been doing, but I really could not have cared less about what god thought of my extracurricular activities.

Still, the shame was there, simmering.

And then somehow I have a boyfriend and it all catches up to me while I am lying on his cream-coloured sheets in his double bed in his room trying not to move and trying to catch my breath.

It is a Sunday.

My next relationship was with M – this was my first 'real' relationship. I met him at work, while tensions between me and my parents were high. He made me feel like I belonged, and his parents were kind to me too – almost too kind. They treated me as if I were part of their family. They weren't afraid to speak their minds, and they talked about sex like it was a normal part of their lives, not something to be avoided or hidden away.

They were all I thought parents should be. They were who I wished my parents could have been when I was younger. In some ways, they were who I wish my parents could be now.

I started to spend more time with them than I did with my own parents.

I didn't tell my parents I was in a relationship for about eight months – and even when the words came out of my mouth, it was only out of necessity. They'd met him before, but only as a friend, so they knew he wasn't Chinese. They didn't explicitly disapprove of the relationship, but I detected touches of disappointment. I never thought of my relationship as wrong or abnormal, but filial piety runs deep.

When I told Dad that I didn't know if M wanted to learn Mandarin, he replied, '你應該找一個想學華文的男朋友,' shaking his head. I thought about defending M, but I didn't. It would have taken too much effort.

In an attempt to assuage my guilt, I tried to teach him a phrase or two. It never lasted. I was too impatient, he could never get the tones right, and I either got frustrated or passive aggressive, so we usually just ended up fucking.

After I moved out of home, I told my parents I was going to a church on my side of town, because I didn't have a car and their church wasn't easily accessible by public transport. Unsurprisingly, I wasn't going to church – I actually spent most of my Sundays at M's house. Ironically, it was almost ritualistic. He was a late riser, so I usually arrived mid-morning. I did the Sunday crossword with his mother – hers on the newspaper itself, mine a photocopied version. We both used blunt 2B pencils and exchanged stories about our weeks. If the cricket was on, I would watch it with his stepdad; if the cat was around, I would play with him until he got sick of me and yowled at me to go away. Sometimes M would come upstairs for a grouchy hello, a kiss, a mug of coffee, and a bite of breakfast. If not, I would take myself downstairs to find him, and we'd hang out – sometimes in his room, sometimes in the living room. We talked, played video games, wrote, watched Netflix, had sex.

I loved the idea of fucking on Sundays. I thought of it as a way of saying fuck you to a god I no longer believed in, as a kind of empowerment, taking my body back from those who had controlled it through my adolescence. I wanted to reclaim it from the values that had policed my clothing choices, to reclaim it from the people who tried to make me feel embarrassed for wanting to show off some skin, for wanting to feel sexy. I wanted to know what it was like to know my body without feeling ashamed, and I wanted to share that with someone else.

But simmering alongside these feelings of empowerment was a growing mass of shame and guilt, powered by filial piety and a lifetime of Christian devotion and rules. I didn't believe in the Christian god anymore, and I wanted to say fuck you to him by fucking someone else, but the impact of childhood Sunday school lessons, hour-long sermons, and weekly Bible study remained embedded in my bones, welded to the lining of my stomach.

*

Our last conversation in person happened before I left for my first Chinese New Year celebration in Malaysia with my extended family. I'd just finished a work shift and M had arrived early for his. We talked about something benign, gave each other a hug and a kiss, and I promised to message him once I'd landed.

Malaysia was ringing in the year of the ram (or lamb or goat or sheep – take your pick), and the shopping centres and roads were lined with red and gold and every imaginable depiction of this animal. I only remembered snippets of the pre-new-year celebrations, because at some point M broke up with me via Facebook Messenger, claiming I was too clingy and needy and that he'd fallen out of love with me.

I was distraught, and I spent days sobbing and trying to reason with him over patchy internet. One day after I woke up, inconsolable, my mother told me, 'Well, we didn't really like him that much, anyway,' before trying to cheer me up by taking me shopping. Her words rolled around in my head, through the aisles of Uniqlo, down the street markets in Kuala Lumpur, into my aunt's front yard in Sarikei where my cousins set off firecrackers to welcome in the new year, and back to Australia, to my apartment in Indooroopilly, where he handed me a box of my things and I still couldn't seem to stop crying.

I don't know if Mum was trying to be comforting, or if she meant I could do better. I wanted her to be supportive, like mums are in television shows and movies when their daughters are dumped for the first time – but maybe this was her version of support. I was taken aback at how seemingly unemotional she was in the face of my continual distress, but this is also the nature of our relationship – we don't reveal ourselves much to each other, if at all.

Maybe she was trying to tell me I should have chosen a Chinese boy. That next time, I should choose a Chinese boy – or even better, a *Christian* Chinese boy. Then everything would work out. Then maybe I wouldn't feel so guilty, because I wouldn't be turning my back on my culture and my upbringing. Maybe when we fuck (after we are married, of course) it'll feel right. The knot won't even make an appearance.

Over the years, the knot has mostly disappeared from my insides. I'd like to think I've unravelled it, but I know this remnant of the rules I internalised throughout my childhood won't ever really be gone. It still shows up occasionally, but usually only as a warning that I might be getting in too deep with the wrong person. Sometimes I wonder if it will disappear if I do all the things I'm supposed to – get married to a good Chinese boy, settle down, have kids. Sometimes I wonder if I could have avoided this whole mess by just listening to my parents and being a good girl. I wonder if I would have been happier, if it would have made any kind of difference.

I prayed after M broke up with me, because I didn't know who or what else to turn to. *Dear God, please make this stop, please make this go away, please make me feel better.* It couldn't hurt, right? I know my parents prayed for me then too, like they probably still do now. I know they pray at church and before all their meals, and sometimes at other people's places if we are visiting for lunch or dinner. I know they pray before they go to bed, but I've never seen or heard them do it. Kind of like sex, I suppose.

I don't believe in the God that I was brought up with anymore, but the idea of being alone in a quiet space with my thoughts is still comforting. Regardless of my faith, I still see church and prayer as places of peace.

In high school, I'd sneak into the chapel during break times when I felt upset, or when the world became a little too overwhelming. I'd sit in one of the wooden pews, right up the back, crumpled in a ball against the rigid oaken seats. Sometimes I stared at the stained-glass windows, and other times I closed my eyes, thankful for the stillness of the space and the chance to get away from everyone and everything. I'd talk to myself – I don't know that I'd necessarily call it praying – and I always left feeling at least a little calmer than I'd been when I first entered.

I can see how prayer has the power to help people, even if it is only a placebo.

Many of my in-depth conversations with my dad have happened in the car – it's the one place for us to have time alone together, without interference from Mum or my sister. In 2013, after I'd just finished a busy shift at Sizzler, I was driving us home. I was sweaty and tired, and the streetlights on Coronation Drive winked encouragingly at me, urging me to stay awake.

I had at least another half-hour of driving ahead of me, most of it on the highway.

I stopped at the set of traffic lights that also marked the turn-off for the Go Between Bridge. Dad was in the front seat, and he had been thinking. He leant forward slightly. He asked me how M was, and I answered with a curt, adolescent 'He's okay.'

'You know, you should never do anything you don't want to do,' he continued. '別人做的東西你不需用做, 你知道嗎? 不要讓朋友 pressure 你做你不要做的事.'

My first reaction was a long internal cackle. He had no idea that I was more than willing to have as much sex as my boyfriend would give me. If only he knew, I scoffed. After the laughter, there was anger, white-hot behind my eyes, because I understood the implication of his words: it's a sin to have sex before you are married. *You don't want to be a sinner, do you?* I felt myself welling up, angry at the insinuation that I was not in control of myself or my relationship, angry that he had brought religion into this, angry at a culture that meant he had to skirt around the subject instead of just saying the word 'sex' so god forbid we could have an honest conversation about it all.

I blinked away the tears, and I was left with a hard, pebble-sized ball that ricocheted off the walls of my stomach, the noise echoing into my ears.

Only seconds had passed, and the laughter and the lights and the anger and the tears and the guilt and the sharp bouncing noise was almost too much, and I realised I needed to respond.

I stared straight ahead, the red of the traffic light blaring into my mind. I gave him what he wanted to hear:

'Yeah, I get it.'

My answer satisfied him. He trusted me. He didn't know any better. We haven't talked about anything related to sex or relationships since.

2

Pleasure

The first time I make a woman orgasm, endorphins flood my brain. She comes on my face as I flick my tongue across her clit, her pussy dripping with my saliva and her desire. Later, she orgasms on my fingers, her hips bucking against my wrist as I curl my fingers inside her. I savour the way she moves, claws at me, sighs into my mouth as she kisses me, the way she *comes*. A wicked grin unfolds across my face as she begs me not to stop even after she's come, and I continue to dig my fingers into her shoulder and her back and her cunt until she moves herself down the bed to kiss me again.

We taste like sex. We are warm, sticky, delicious. I can see where the analogies to warm toffee pudding come from, even though she doesn't taste like any kind of pudding I've ever tried. She tastes like pussy. And all I can think is *I want more* – it's irresistible. I've never felt this way before – the aftermath of a man's orgasm is so different, and all men come in pretty much the same way. I want to explore other women's bodies. I want to know what makes them tick, what sounds they'll make if I touch here or press there or kiss here. I want them to explore my body; I want to see the smiles on their faces as they make me squeal or moan or clutch at the bedsheets like I'm hanging on for dear life.

'Being able to come from penetration is a kind of superpower,' I say, when we're both in the shower afterwards. She shrugs – not dismissively, but she's also shivering a little and wants me to stop hogging the water. I wish it was easier for me to come, to surrender and to relax, if only for a few seconds. She smiles at me and I shuffle aside. Then she pulls me close and whispers in my ear, 'I can't wait to do this again.'

I learnt about orgasms from a crime novel – one of those paperbacks that looked as if it came from the two-dollar table at the local newsagent. I don't know how it came to be in the house in the first place, but there it sat on the living-room bookshelf next to the television, nestled among my mum's well-loved copies of *The Famous Five* and *The Secret Seven*.

Sex wasn't the focus of that crime novel, but the only thing I remember about it were the passages that described a woman enjoying herself tremendously during sex. Even though the word 'orgasm' wasn't explicitly mentioned, I knew what the words were trying to convey. This woman experienced body-shuddering convulsions of pleasure courtesy of one particular man's sexual prowess, and I read these passages over and over, trying to sear these images into my brain.

I knew about sex before this point, of course. I knew my first time was supposed to hurt. *It's not magical like the movies would have you believe*, I was counselled, by high school friends who seemed more worldly than I ever could be. *It's going to be messy, and it probably won't be great. It's okay, though, because it gets better.* I was young and naive, and I trusted that my friends knew what they were talking about. I'd probably also watched a little too much *Grey's Anatomy*, and I knew all the ways things could go wrong.

I'd heard all sorts of things about sex and how it was 'supposed' to be, but it never crossed my mind that sex would be something I'd have to endure. I've had my fair share of sex, and sometimes it's been mediocre, but it's never been traumatic. I've always seen sex as something fun, something pleasurable – a physical, if momentary, distraction from the realities of life outside my bedroom. After M broke up with me, I used sex as an easy way to access endorphins and adrenaline. I rode the somewhat manufactured high for a year – maybe more – until I realised I was wasting my time on dating apps chasing something that wasn't really doing it for me anymore.

Even now, the word 'masturbate' looks dirty to me. I think it's because of the u that's right in the middle of the word. It's too open, too vagina-like. Or maybe it's just because of the messaging and conditioning I've been subject to over the past twenty-odd years of my life – messaging we've all been exposed to, whether we like it or not.

Funnily enough, I discovered the joys of masturbation by accident. In primary school, I climbed poles in the playground by wrapping my legs around them and pulling myself up. I learnt to do this primarily so I could hang from the high bar and try to do flips and somersaults off the monkey bars. But I also found that if I rested my pelvis against the pole, clung to it, and kept up the climbing action, a nice kind of warmth would spread throughout my body – a warmth I'd never felt before, and a warmth I wanted to hold on to for as long as possible. I clung to a lot of poles during primary school, my thighs desperately chasing that high, past the morning tea and lunch bells, unaware that I was basically masturbating in public.

During this time, I read everything I could get my hands on, and this included Mum's stash of *Good Medicine* magazines. While I waited for Mum to finish work, I scoured these from cover to cover after school, especially if I'd finished all the books I'd borrowed from the library. Naturally, there were sections about improving your sex life (though it was always stated in more euphemistic terms), but they rarely used the terms 'vulva' or 'vagina' outright. Even though there were 'tips and tricks' or suggestions, I couldn't follow them properly, because I didn't know what was going on when it came to my anatomy.

The only information I had at the time was a vague mention of 'women have three holes, while men only have two' in a sex education class without any further explanation. This was during the time of dial-up internet, so I looked for a diagram of the female genital area in the library – I think it was in one of those DK anatomy books – hoping no-one would see me or ask me what I was doing. It was all very clinical, diagrams in shades of red and nude and orange, but it was from this diagram that I learnt of something called 'the clitoris'. I learnt that it had a hood, and if you pulled the hood back a little then you'd find a place tingling with nerve endings. I learnt it was one of the most sensitive places, if not the most sensitive place on the human body.

And so I played around with my clit. I didn't not like the feeling it gave me, but I was crippled by the notion that I might be 'doing it wrong', and that was on top of the feeling that what I was doing *was* wrong in the first place. I worried that anyone I asked would laugh and make fun of me for my lack of knowledge, so I kept my investigation a secret. It took me a while to figure out how it all worked – how much pressure I liked and where. I worked out how much was too much, how to tone it down or to amp it up, how to keep myself on the edge for just that bit longer before succumbing to my body's needs.

But before I introduced myself to the wonders of masturbation-via-clitoris, I had already tried to simulate penetrative sex. I was probably nine or ten during my first attempts, but this experimentation carried on until I was well into my mid-teens. I barely got any pocket money as a child, and while I was at school I wasn't allowed to get a job – so I had to get inventive. I looked for small cylindrical items around the house that I thought I could put inside myself easily. Solutions came in many forms: mini shampoo bottles with string around their lids so I could retrieve them if they ever got stuck too deep, Vicks VapoRub sticks (with the cover on, of course), electric toothbrushes. Once I tried to stick a carrot ensconced in cling wrap inside myself – the logic being that the plastic made it somehow more hygienic, and that I could also return the carrot to its rightful place in the vegetable crisper when I was done. (I ended up putting the whole thing in the bin.)

During my first few attempts, I wasn't even inserting anything into my vagina – I'd got the wrong hole and was fucking my arse instead. I also didn't know about toy cleaner, so I washed my makeshift toys with water and soap. Looking back, I could have done myself serious harm if anything had gone wrong, and I'm sure many other young people have had similar experiences.

After much experimentation, I found that the most reliable way to get an orgasm (or something approximating an orgasm) during this time was using the good old electric toothbrush – a trick I gleaned off the internet one day during a hasty incognito search. I wonder what my parents would have thought if they'd walked in on me lying on the shower tiles, my knees in the air, my feet braced against the shower door and wall, the toothbrush whirring away between my legs. In typical teenager fashion, I thought I was being clever – running the shower extra loud, and locking the door even though I wasn't supposed to and my sister knew the secret to jimmying the lock. In hindsight, they could probably hear the toothbrush over the running water, and the fact that

I was regularly spending over ten minutes in the shower was probably also a sign that something was going on. Or maybe they were just in denial.

As I grew older, I became bolder. If I was ever alone in the house, I would take the electric toothbrush and a spare brush head, lie on the bed in the spare room, and let it run until I felt my inner thighs run flush with blood, until my body started to make small, involuntary movements that I couldn't control. I worried about where to hide the spare brush head, what I'd do if I wore it out, how long it would take me to run to the other side of the house and pretend everything was okay once I heard the rumbling of the garage door. I don't know what I would have said if I'd ever been caught and what my parents' reaction would have been, but I'm still glad I had a fast reaction time and a plan of attack. My masturbatory adventures in that big empty house gave me my first taste of freedom – of being in control of my body and my sexual pleasure. I was able to be as loud as I wanted while I did whatever I wanted, a concept that was foreign to me at the time.

More than a decade later, with the cumulative knowledge born from many years of experience and safe experimentation, I know masturbation is something of an art. It's usually easier and faster if I have something that vibrates, but even then it's not such a straightforward process. Porn helps, but I don't need it. I have to use my base understanding of what works for me personally – which areas are more sensitive, which areas are uncomfortable, how much is too much, which movements will help and which ones will hinder – but it's still not cut and dried. Sometimes it might take me five minutes to come; other times it might take me thirty-five.

Figuring all this out has taken years of practice – I don't come easily, and especially not from penetration. I'm fairly unconvinced the G-spot works or exists, but that might just be my body. I can come from clitoral stimulation, but only if the right amount of pressure is applied alongside the right movements – or, alternatively, if a vibrator is strapped to my clit.

My experiences aren't out of the ordinary. A majority of cis women can't orgasm reliably as a result of intercourse, and an even smaller percentage can orgasm reliably as a result of penetrative sex. This information wasn't readily available to me when I was in my late teens, and I wonder if my attitude towards orgasms and pleasure would have been different if I had known this earlier. Research conducted in the United States in 2016 shows that 95 per cent of straight men orgasm during sex, compared to 86 per cent of lesbian women and just 65 per cent of straight women – this means women are significantly less likely to orgasm during sex with a man.[1] Disappointingly few studies have been done when it comes to trans people and orgasms, but I'd hazard a guess that they also experience orgasms at a rate far lower than straight men.

When I first started having sex, I promised myself I wouldn't fake an orgasm. To do so would be unfair to both him and me, I thought. I'd be lying to him *and* cheating myself out of something I also deserved. But that was before I started dating men, many of whom seem to have an almost unhealthy preoccupation with orgasms, whether it be their own or mine.

So ... I have faked orgasms. I've faked them because I'm tired and I want to go to sleep, because I want the guy to stop banging on about how he's always been able to give the best orgasms, how he sees me as a challenge because he's never met a girl he couldn't make come.

I harbour a special derision for men who pride themselves on how fast they can make a woman orgasm, or who like to mention how many times they've made a woman come in one night. Once, just to spite a guy who wouldn't stop complaining about how I hadn't come, I lay on the bed beside him and gave myself an orgasm, screams and all. It was worth it for the look on his face afterwards.

Orgasms are great, but they shouldn't be the sole focus of sex; sex shouldn't be seen as 'bad' or 'failed' just because an orgasm isn't involved – though in my experience, that certainly doesn't stop men from trying, even after it's obvious it's not going to happen.

But when I'm fucking, I'm not chasing an orgasm. I'm chasing an experience, and hopefully some sort of connection. I don't orgasm often, but I still love the cadence of foreplay and sex, the way it can alternate, the way it makes my body hum – that's why I keep having it, that's why I keep those god-forsaken dating apps on my phone.

I've done my fair share of dating, and dating *around* – I actually met my current partner through Tinder. He has a big television screen in his bedroom, and sometimes, when we're fucking, he asks if I want to watch him fuck me on the screen. I always say yes, and it's always a huge turn-on. Afterwards, I feel like I've been self-indulgent, too selfish. But I've always loved watching. I begged to be fucked in front of my ex's mirror, my knees burning on carpet as I watched him move in and out of me. I love it when the hotel room I've booked has a giant mirror next to the bed because I know I'll only need to turn my head slightly to the side to watch my back ripple and curve as I ride my partner.

I've never watched myself orgasm, though. I've watched in the mirror as I've teased myself, fingers circling gently around my clit, my chest rising a little higher and dipping a little deeper as my arousal heightens. But I can't bring myself to open my eyes when that wave hits me – it's almost like I need them closed to feel the full weight of my orgasm. Maybe some things are best left unseen.

I am, however, in a slightly narcissistic way, turned on by the sounds I make when I'm fucking. I used to be embarrassed by it, the fact I couldn't keep my damned mouth shut. I was afraid people would think I was faking my enthusiasm, that I sounded too much like a porn star, that they wouldn't want to have sex with me again because I'd wake up their housemates or the neighbours. I used to worry that I'd reinforce the idea of the hypersexual Asian woman if I made too much noise.

Contrary to the beliefs of some partners, I can keep quiet if I want to, or if the situation calls for it – for example, a semi-private open-air onsen at eleven at night – but I like being loud. I like to communicate my pleasure.

Like many Chinese women, I was raised to be quiet and obedient. In most situations, I still prefer to sit back and stay silent. I shouldn't bother others, even when I'm clearly enjoying myself. I shouldn't impose. Sometimes I hate that I play right into the stereotype. I know I am more than what people think of me, but it is hard to break free from something you've been told your whole life, even if it is in the privacy of your own bed.

In 'What Does It Mean to Be Durational, Not Eternal?', the first poem in *Careen* (Noemi Press, 2019), Grace Shuyi Liew's debut poetry collection, she writes, 'I can't be loud/ when Asian porn is still/a consumer category'.[2] This feeling of shame, of being constantly fetishised, is pervasive. It's often felt by women who look like me, while the perpetrators of such fetishisation face no consequences for their actions – and it is paralysing. It's difficult to find the energy to fight for a semblance of personhood when there are those who still see my face and my body as an object of capitalism. And so we are hushed, made to feel small, simply by virtue of who we are, by virtue of the ways in which our existence has affected and 'tempted' the men around us.

When Vi Khi Nao asks her about this line in an interview for the *LA Review of Books*, Liew says, 'I wanted to please and be pleased, but was horrified about being a site of pleasure. I could not disentangle where my private desires ended and where a public projection began.'[3] This intermingling of the public and private, exacerbated by the prevalence of social media, culminates in a blending of boundaries. For me, this presented itself, in part, through an intense feeling of guilt and shame as a teenager after masturbating – even more so if I let a moan or a gasp slip, even if I knew no-one else was around to hear me.

I don't know how conscious I was of this shame, but it was there – born of a combination of conservative family and cultural values and society's disdain for women's pleasure. A study conducted in 2014 for the Second Australian Study of Health and Relationships showed that just under one in four women masturbated in the past four weeks, and just under one in two women masturbated in the past year.[4] The same study also noted that people who came from religious backgrounds and those who did not speak English at home were generally less likely to masturbate. These statistics, while shocking, are unsurprising. As the ASHR is only conducted every ten years, it will be interesting to see if these figures have changed when the results of the next iteration of this study are released later in 2023. There are a multitude of forces working together to shame women out of masturbation, out of a pleasure that is for them and them alone.

Communicating pleasure is easier if you know what's causing it, and that's where cliteracy comes in. Sophia Wallace, an American conceptual artist, has been promoting cliteracy since

2013, and insists her work is for everyone, not just people who have a clitoris. It's a 'metaphor for freedom, body sovereignty and citizenship', she says. 'Cliteracy is about not having one's body controlled or legislated. Not having access to the pleasure that is your birthright is a deeply political act.'[5] As I read these words, I realised it was the first time I'd heard someone explicitly state the political ramifications of owning my own pleasure.

Wallace's artwork *CLITERACY, 100 Natural Laws* features a series of facts and debunked myths about the clitoris in block letters, like 'society idealizes male genitals while teaching girls that their genitals are grotesque, shameful, yet the nexus of their worth',[6] and is a striking visual representation of the sheer volume of misinformation out there on women's sexual pleasure. However, my favourite of Wallace's work has to be Άδάμας, which she claims is the 'first anatomically correct sculpture of the clitoris'.[7] Standing at just over a metre tall, and made from wood, fibreglass, steel, and enamel, it was originally meant to hang from the ceiling. But as Wallace developed the work, she realised she 'wanted the sculpture to stand face to face with viewers. To be viewed as a subject after being absent for so long.'[8]

Over the years, programs that promote cliteracy have spread into more mainstream and accessible outlets. 'The Female Orgasm', an episode of Netflix's *Explained* series, discusses how common it is for women to never have had an orgasm during sex with a man, and corrects myths about the clitoris and women's orgasms.[9] *Oh Joy Sex Toy*, a free weekly sex education and sex toy reviewing webcomic drawn by

Erika and Matt, who are queer and bi respectively, is another fantastically welcoming and accessible resource. The comics are fun, committed to representation, and are not clinical at all. In their guide to masturbating, the clitoris is drawn as a smiling pea, and there's an image of a smiling woman gliding down a wave with the caption 'generally speaking, a slippery vulva is a happy vulva'[10] alongside a diagram of a vulva that hasn't been smoothed out or made to look unrealistic. There are guest artists, too, and the website is full of comics about vaginosis, periods, vasectomies, asexuality, menopause, how to orgasm, anal sex, non-monogamy, and much more. It's such a supportive environment, and recognises that navigating these issues can be sensitive for many people regardless of age.

These resources should be more readily available, and they should be able to be shared widely without fear of censorship. If I could have accessed these when I was a teenager, it probably would have prevented me from enacting my potentially dangerous night-time experiments. I would still have been an awkward, nerdy, quiet girl, but I wouldn't have been so afraid to ask questions about sex, because I would have known more about it to begin with.

Despite the uptick in programs and resources around cliteracy, the majority of the faces involved in this work are white. If I had been brave enough to try to talk about any of this with my mother – even as an adult – she'd most likely have brushed it off with a comment like '那是外國人的想法, 我們華人不會講這種的話.' In a sense, she's right. White people are more open when it comes to speaking about sex and sexuality, and there are nuances to non-white women's experiences around sex, masturbation, and even how to interact with people of another gender – especially when combined with differences in language, race, and culture – that can be difficult for white women to understand. I want women who look like me to be talking and writing and singing and painting and making more art about sex in the public sphere.

The Principles of Pleasure, another Netflix series, is a step in the right direction.[11] The show discusses everything from anatomy to consent and trauma and the impacts of colonisation, featuring the voices of a genuinely diverse set of women. Interviews are interspersed with animations, both of which feature women of colour, fat women, trans women, and women with disabilities. I loved seeing Julia Zou and Supriya Ganesh on screen, unafraid to talk about their experiences around sex. The show is, however, like many such programs, very much reflective of an American mindset – there are subtleties to living between cultures that cannot be explored in three short episodes.

Women's sexual pleasure – or rather, its blatant promotion – has also been a subject of controversy in the burgeoning innovation and technology sector. In January 2019, Lora DiCarlo's hands-free sex toy, the Osé personal massager, was awarded the Consumer Electronics Show (CES) Innovation Award, before being stripped of its title. As *New York Times* journalist Valeriya Safronova reported, 'a representative cited a clause in the awards' terms and conditions that disqualified products deemed "immoral, obscene, indecent, profane, or not keeping in with CTA [the Consumer Technology Association]'s image".[12] This decision was made despite the fact that many male sex toys – or rather, products aimed at increasing male sexual pleasure – had been previously exhibited at CES, with some even winning the same prize as the Osé personal massager. CES later released a statement to *The New York Times* stating the product 'did not fit into the robotics and drones category, nor into any of the other product categories',[13] which many, including those involved in the development of the toy, strongly dispute.

The disparity between the treatment of men's and women's sexual pleasure is further highlighted by the fact that older renditions of CES commonly featured scantily clad 'booth babes' promoting a range of products, including earphones, an app with the ability to enhance sound quality in any set of headphones,[14] and gaming gear like headsets and keyboards.[15] HyperShop, an electronics accessories company, went one step further in 2013, when they hired women covered only in body paint to promote their newest product: a battery pack.[16] Additionally, Fiera, a device that assisted in enhancing libido, was rejected in 2015, and a smart vibrator for women from Lioness was rejected in 2017. In an open letter to CES, Lora Haddock, the CEO of Lora DiCarlo, notes that the show allowed a sex doll, with the creepy name 'Harmony', to be displayed in 2018. She also writes of rooms allocated each year for people (mainly men) to watch virtual reality porn, and flags that none of these were deemed 'immoral, obscene, indecent, [or] profane'. Haddock concludes by calling out CTA's comfort with 'allowing explicit male sexuality and pleasure to be ostentatiously on display [...] but apparently there is something different, something threatening about Osé, a product created by women to empower women'.[17]

This seeming 'threat' of women's sexual pleasure – of men possibly being rendered obsolete – is also reflected in the products that receive awards at CES. Lora DiCarlo's technical director, Lola Vars, mentions that OhMiBod, a Kegel exerciser, won an award at CES in 2016, not solely because of its potential contribution towards sexual wellness for women, but because it's also good for men. 'It's something construed as good for men's pleasure or fertility,' she says in an interview for Safronova's article. 'I hear that as a joke from men: "I like to sleep with women who do their Kegels."'[18] It may just be a joke, but there is an implication here that women are responsible for men's sexual pleasure, possibly to the detriment of their own.

It is upsetting that in this day and age, a product that's supposed to help with continence and the strengthening of a woman's pelvic floor – which, admittedly, has positive implications when it comes to women's sexual pleasure and wellness – has to be paired with an equal benefit for men to be worthy of note. Better sex alone means better sex with others, and we should all be free to learn about our own bodies and what works best for us at our own pace, using whatever tools we want. Women's pleasure, shockingly, *can* stand alone, as my collection of vibrators (including one from Lora DiCarlo) will testify. If corporations – especially those who claim to be at the forefront of technological innovation – don't want to alienate half of their potential client base, they'd better get on board *fast*.

One day, my partner showed me a Reddit post where someone had written, *A man's orgasm is required for the purposes of reproduction, a woman's isn't – so why do women need to enjoy sex at all?* It's an idea I've seen expressed every so often on Twitter. This statement teeters dangerously into condoning sexual assault, which is troubling in and of itself, and it's also clear that men who hold these sorts of opinions do not care about women's sexual pleasure – or women in general. But the truly dangerous part of this statement lies in its implications for consent.

Men, especially those who have internalised ideals of hypermasculinity, have been shown to conflate pleasure with consent, and to be more likely to confuse sexual desire with consent. Richard Mattson and Ashton Lofgreen's study of 145 American college students in 2017 reported that 'ratings of women's sexual desire and consent were so highly correlated that these responses were effectively indistinguishable'.[19] This is reflected in comments like 'she was enjoying it, so it couldn't have been rape', or 'she didn't say no, so it couldn't have been rape', which often crop up when discussing cases of sexual assault, even when the woman was clearly incapacitated. Such sentiments are then given legitimacy when courts find in favour of the rapist – Andrea Constand's abuser walked free in 2021 after having his conviction overturned – or otherwise deliver sentences that clearly do not match the severity of the crimes the accused have been found guilty of committing – Chanel Miller's rapist only served ninety days in jail.

At its basest level, these cases tell men it's okay to commit acts of sexual assault against women because they either don't acknowledge it as such, or do so with the knowledge that they will probably get away with it. In an open letter regarding the strategy for the prevention of violence against women and children written in 2021, Angela Lynch, the chief executive of the Queensland Woman's Legal Service, notes that every year in Australia, 'it is estimated there are between 20,000 to 40,000 rapes and sexual assaults. However, only 6,500 charges are laid and 300 findings of guilt and guilty pleas each year. This equates to a 1.5% conviction rate but is likely worse.'[20] All these factors contribute to an environment where women are less willing to come forward with their experiences of sexual assault, or even to admit to themselves that they may have been sexually assaulted.

This is complicated further by the fact that some see a direct relationship between supposed pleasure and consent. A study published in the *Journal of Experimental Psychology* asked participants to read a number of scenarios involving different types of sexual encounters, before judging the level of distress that would have been experienced in each scenario. They were then asked if they considered the scenario to be sexual assault. The study found that 'Wantedness and pleasure […] influenced whether participants considered the situation rape in nonconsensual scenarios',[21] showing a disregard for the reasons why a woman would fake pleasure when placed in such scenarios. I'm lucky to have never been sexually assaulted, but I have pretended to enjoy myself during sex just so I could get rid of a guy who I felt was being a bit shady – and I'm sure I'm not the only woman to have had this sort of experience.

Toxic masculinity and sexism also play a role here; the researchers of this study stated, 'Male participants and those higher in benevolent sexism were more likely than women to utilize pleasure and wantedness in judging whether situations described rape.'[22] Given the number of white men in positions of power, especially among judges and government officials, it's no wonder these attitudes persist. As a society, we need to widen our discussions around pleasure and consent, and expand them beyond the purely biological. Women should feel free to enjoy sex as much as they want and to express this in whatever way they see fit – and they should also feel confident enough to be heard, loud and clear, when their boundaries have been crossed.

It's not uncommon for women to declare their ownership of their personal pleasure through bumper stickers and posters that proclaim a love for vibrators. I've also seen it in many a television or movie scene, but my favourite instance of a woman enjoying the sexual freedom that comes with having a vibrator has to be in Michelle Law's *Single Asian Female*. The first time I saw this play I was tired and cranky – my flight back to Brisbane from Melbourne had been delayed for more than two hours and I spent that whole time afraid that I'd miss opening night – but it didn't dampen my enthusiasm for the production. One of my favourite scenes features Pearl, who would probably be my mother's age, declaring, 'All of the women here should know that in this modern age, the world is your oyster. And you definitely do not need a man in that oyster. There is such thing as a vibrator.'[23] She then climbs onto a restaurant table, finishing the scene by belting out the last lines of 'I Will Survive'. Watching this scene was another first for me – the first time I'd ever heard a Chinese auntie talk about vibrators.

I want to hear more Asian women talk about vibrators and reclaiming their sexual pleasure from the hands of creepy white men. I want them to have the confidence to talk about this with each other, but also with their daughters and nieces and granddaughters. I want us to be more open about it all, to not be afraid to ask each other for help or advice. I hope I will be brave enough to be one of those Chinese aunties in the future.

In her interview about *Careen* in the *LA Review of Books*, Grace Shuyi Liew tells Vi Khi Nao:

> I want our [Asian women's] literary and cultural lineages to be filled with heartbreaks that do not either kill us off or make us holier; I want to see us flawed and susceptible to every vice and desirous of every perfection. I want coming-of-age narratives in which pain and melancholy are not the sole vehicles for our character development. I want our desires to undo us only if we let it, and not as de facto punishment for greed.[24]

Liew argues for something even bigger, more radical, than just independence. It's a call to reclaim and reform the values that have pushed us into the boxes we inhabit today, especially those that have been pushed onto Black and brown and Indigenous and Asian women by the rice-porridge sludge that is the patriarchy. Liew's words strike to the heart of how I feel about myself, my pleasure, my story, how I want this book to be read.

I want other Asian girls and women to be at least a little more comfortable talking about sex – the good, the bad, and the ugly, and everything in between. It's hard to do this when so few others are doing it too, but the few who do have been massive inspirations. Reading work by essayist Shu-Ling Chua and writer Giselle Au-Nhien Nguyen, in particular, made (and still makes) me feel seen. In 'Them Spitting Eels', Chua writes:

> I am the girl my mother said to watch out for.
> The type of girl who has sex before marriage, and writes
>   about it.
> I never expected I'd be this girl.[25]

I, too, never thought I'd be here. But somehow, it feels right.

I've read plenty of erotica since that two-dollar newsagent crime novel, but it wasn't until I picked up Larissa Pham's *Fantasian* (Badlands Unlimited, 2016) on a friend's recommendation that I truly felt seen in this genre. The unnamed protagonist, of (East-)Asian descent, is in a relationship with Astrid, a rich white woman, when she meets Dolores, a woman who seems to look exactly like her. During the course of the story, the protagonist has something of an awakening – not just sexually, but also in regards to Astrid and class and race and her place in the world. In a conversation with Dolores, the protagonist mentions that '[Astrid] has no idea that other people's realities differ from hers, or that the world was built to accommodate only certain kinds of people', and that she feels like a sort of 'POC sidequest'[26] in Astrid's life. She also expresses relief at being able to talk to someone who understands what she's feeling. 'Sometimes I feel crazy for all the things I think I'm noticing and feeling,'[27] she says, and as someone who tries hard not to be *that* person who makes everything about race, even when it obviously *is* about race, I empathise deeply with her.

Like many readers who have been raised in the West, or who have grown up consuming predominantly Western literature, I automatically construct a white character in my head if the character's race isn't explicitly mentioned. In the case of *Fantasian*, I knew the character was of Asian descent, and so this was the first time I read a sex scene with an Asian character in mind. As the protagonist prepares to masturbate, she says:

> I angle myself so I can see my reflection and, shit, it's really hot. I forgot what it was like to make eye contact with myself, my fingers on my pulsing clit, then slipping to where the moisture is beginning to form, tracing shallow circles around the entrance to my cunt, not yet ready to penetrate myself ...[28]

I could be this woman, I thought. She likes it rough; 'It's what I want,' she says, when she's fucking a guy, 'Even how it hurts, especially how it hurts.'[29] I read on for a little longer, before catching myself and returning to that revolutionary thought: *I could* really *be this woman.* It's a startling thought to have for the first time at twenty-five, despite a life of voracious reading, which included numerous sex scenes in a variety of fantastical worlds where magic was real and so was intergalactic travel and children were trained to fly on dragons while also being tasked with saving the world but sex involving women of Asian descent was a little too far-fetched.

Pham's novella depicts all kinds of sex – sex with men, sex with women, blowjobs, fingering, eating pussy, masturbation with and without the help of a toy, a threesome. It explores what it is to be a sexual being – not a sexual*ised* being – while also teasing apart issues of race and class. No judgement is passed on the protagonist for the fact that she likes having sex, or that she has a lot of sex. The type of sex she enjoys and how she fucks isn't related to her Asianness. Sex is simply something she does and enjoys, just as it is for countless Asian women around the world – just as it has always been in novels featuring white women.

Fantasian ends with a fire, initiated by the protagonist/ Dolores – it's unclear who is who at this point, as the protagonist, at Dolores's request, has been pretending to be Dolores for nearly a week. The fire is 'incandescent'; according to some witnesses, it burns quickly through the sixth floor of the building the apartment is in after ripping apart the apartment itself. It is a climax of sorts, and reminds me of the scene at the end of Jean Rhys's *Wide Sargasso Sea* (W. W. Norton & Company, 1966) when Bertha (Antoinette) Mason burns down Thornfield Hall. Antoinette, who has been imprisoned by and subjected to the whims of the white man for the entire novel, is happiest at this point – after she has lit the fire, and just before she dies. The reader, especially if they have read *Jane Eyre* (Penguin, 1847), knows the entirety of *Wide Sargasso Sea* has been leading up to this moment, the moment when Antoinette burns down the coloniser's house; in essence, the climax of the novel for both reader and protagonist.

Even though these two fires start under different circumstances, they are willingly and knowingly lit by women of colour. For both, this is an act of rebellion, a taking of things into their own hands. It is born of a desire to be free, an idea that is still revolutionary in this day and age, especially for a woman or a non-binary person.

I devour *Fantasian* in one sitting. The next time I make myself orgasm, I focus on the feeling of blood rushing into my thighs. I savour its warmth, my body vibrating ever so slightly. I feel beads of sweat running down my legs; I feel like my veins are on fire, burning with pressure and blood and my need – and then it is time to relax and let go, and I arch my back and lift my hips off the bed and the fire in my veins is replaced with what I can only describe as pleasure: liquid, golden, and *mine*.

3

Kink

A set of clover clamps are attached to my nipples. The chain that connects them is pressure sensitive – pulling on it causes the clamps themselves to tighten even further, to bite more greedily into my skin. My arms are bound above my head, and I have been tied in such a way that every tiny movement I make causes a corresponding tug on the clamps. I am unbalanced, on purpose: in order to stop myself from falling over, I must submit to a jolt of pain.

Over the next fifteen minutes, I quiver simultaneously with pain and pleasure. It sounds strange, even unfathomable, but in those moments I am at peace. My brain has stopped spinning at a million miles an hour. I am focused on *now*.

I raise my eyes. There is a twinkle and a curl in my partner's lip – thoughtful, as opposed to malicious – a watchfulness in his eye. *Do you trust me?* he seems to be asking. But no sound comes from his mouth. He doesn't say anything; he just watches.

Finally, he says, 'You suffer so beautifully for me.'

I know.

There is something about being watched like this that turns me on. I've tried to come up with the words to explain why and how, but I always come up empty.

He smiles again, and strokes my hair.

I let out a moan. It is soft, drawn out, and comes from somewhere deep inside my chest.

I trust you.

My interest in kink may have started with an episode of *CSI: Miami*. I remember David Caruso walking out of a building while taking off his sunglasses, and I also remember that, at some point, the investigators walk into a strip club flashing with neon lights and blasting with music. On stage, a series of scantily clad women are pouring honey on their bodies, and there are men in suits licking this honey off them. I think the crime in question was solved by some clue that was related to the type of honey being used, but by the end of the episode I wasn't focused so much on the killer as much as on how it would feel to have someone lick honey off my own body.

I was eight or nine at the time. I didn't really know what was going on, but I knew that watching that scene and replaying it over and over in my head made me feel *something*. On some level, I knew this feeling was wrong, shameful. But I wanted more.

Later, I would learn that having honey poured on your body and licked off isn't actually fun – it's just sticky, requires a long shower afterwards, and is a good way to get a yeast infection if any of it gets in your vagina. But for some reason, that fantasy still remains.

I carried a desire for this experience and others like it through my adolescent years, unaware my interest in kink would manifest itself soon after I started having sex. I wanted to be hit, hard. I savoured the pain, rode the endorphin high, and kept coming back for more. It was almost primal, veering on dangerous. There were times when I thought I was abnormal, because I didn't understand why I so badly wanted to be hurt – surely it wasn't right that I would willingly submit to and enjoy pain being inflicted on me.

G – the boy in the share house in St Lucia – was one of the first people to indulge my fledgling interest in kink. He worked at a hardware store, and sometimes he'd suggest using his staff discount to get some rope so he could tie me to a chair and fuck me. Much to my dismay, this never happened while we were seeing each other.

The first time he bit me, I felt a sharp pain – his teeth sunk into my skin, just beneath my breastbone. I yelped, a mix of surprise and pleasure, and he pinned my arms down. I could almost hear the capillaries breaking, the blood rushing – and then he released me, and I waited for the endorphins to flood my system. His bites were always impossibly round, and I watched over the next couple of days as my blood pooled and blossomed beneath my skin into a purple-red bruise, then as the purples and reds melted into greens and yellows. 'A mark to remember me by,' he'd say.

I always savoured the pain and the endorphins, a heady mixture of hormones I got to keep with me until I got home. The bruises would usually fade before I saw him again, a fresh canvas for him to explore. Sometimes, I'd feel a pang of sadness as they disappeared, but I knew this was the way my body was supposed to work. Bruises were supposed to fade, because the broken capillaries under my skin would eventually release the blood that was making this kaleidoscope of changing colours; this was how my body fixed itself. One of them lasted for months. It stayed, loud and angry, just above my ribs – a perfect circle, an imprint of his mouth. Every time I showered, I marvelled at its roundness.

I'm still a big fan of bruises: they're a sign I can tolerate – have tolerated – pain. I still love being bitten during sex, too. And thanks to my foray into kink, I would learn of myriad other ways to be hurt and to heal.

I wasn't in the kink scene when *Fifty Shades of Grey* became a worldwide sensation, but I certainly heard about it – it would have been hard not to. While I was working at Sizzler, an older, male manager recommended it to me, and more than once. He told me he'd only started reading it because his wife liked it, but he'd also ended up liking it, that it had 'spiced things up' in the bedroom, and that I should try it out too. (Later, he admitted he was having marriage difficulties, and that he was also quite attracted to me.) I tried to read it, to see what the fuss was all about, but I couldn't get past the first couple of pages. I read enough criticism of the book to understand the grave errors in its depiction of dominant/submissive relationships in BDSM, and how it was exceptionally damaging to those in the BDSM community. I ignored the subsequent releases of the second and third books in the trilogy, though I am told they are as bad as, if not worse than, the first.

The first book in the *Fifty Shades* trilogy was released in the same year as Rihanna's song 'S&M', which was criticised in some circles for being too sexually provocative. In the chorus, she explicitly mentions the word 'sex', and adapts the age-old adage 'sticks and stones may break my bones' to declare her interest in chains and whips. Rihanna herself has admitted to having a submissive side in bed. In an interview with *Rolling Stone*, she says, 'I like to take charge, but I love to be submissive [...] You get to be a little lady, to have somebody be macho and in charge of your shit.'[1] This description of power exchange is an example of the connections that can be formed through kink. It should never be one person 'taking advantage' of another – consent on the part of all participants is required. Submission should be given willingly, and never taken non-consensually.

I didn't listen to much commercial radio at the time, but the song eventually filtered its way to me. I remember telling myself I didn't relate to the lyrics at all for a bit – *I'm not really into whips* – but there was no use in denying a part of me that had been active for a while already. Courtesy of a conservative upbringing, an atmosphere of fear around sex, and a society that still considered women who enjoyed having a lot of sex as sluts, I was afraid to admit to myself that I liked sex, and that I liked kinky sex – the kinkier the better.

In the same *Rolling Stone* article, Rihanna mentions she likes to be spanked and that 'being tied up is fun' (Rihanna and I agree on both these points). However, she also says, 'I do think I'm a bit of a masochist [...] It's not something I'm proud of, and it's not something I noticed until recently.'[2] I'm curious as to why she's not proud of being a masochist, even though she's had no problem talking about what she likes to do during sex. Maybe it's because it means the men she gets involved with think they can be more violent or inflict more pain. Or maybe it has something to do with those pesky social norms that have been inflicted upon us by an ever-judgemental patriarchy that never ceases to pounce on anything that could be possibly interpreted as weakness.

The kink scene in Brisbane is relatively small and, like any other community, it has its annoyances and scandals, as well as its charms and redeeming qualities. Politics abounds, and since joining there have been times where I feel like I've been dropped back into high school. I try not to get swept up in it, but like most people I can't resist a tidbit or two of gossip.

My partner, who has been involved in kink since his late

teens, was my gateway into the scene. He told me that even though some might consider those in the kink community as somehow more enlightened, at the end of the day it was 'just a bunch of normal people who are into whips and stuff'. One friend posted a tweet recently that said, *people who are into bdsm and serious kink stuff act like they're exploring the outer realms of human experience but are really just sex nerds having nerd sex.* I haven't been in the kink scene for long, but I've been to enough events and spoken to enough people to know that these words very much ring true.

The kink scene is loosely tied together by people meeting at events and making connections over FetLife, a social media platform for kinksters. It's usually found through 'munches' (casual public events, usually at a pub or a cafe), or through an introduction from someone who's already part of the scene. The community at large is quite good at looking after and looking out for each other, especially when it comes to newbies, but, unfortunately, predators still exist in these spaces.

They can be difficult to catch, because the kink scene sees itself as an all-inclusive, safe space for many who might not feel included or safe in mainstream society. My partner told me of a charismatic man who had been preying on young women for over a decade, creating an almost cult-like community where women would be blackmailed into staying quiet about their experiences. Of course, many people outside of this circle knew he was dangerous and would warn others against playing with him or going to the events he hosted, but there was never enough *proof* that this was what he was doing – it was only ever one person's word against another's. He was only eventually outed because a woman who had nothing to lose called out his behaviour, a woman who insisted he be held accountable for what he had done to her.

Navigating such fraught issues is even harder as a woman of colour, especially in a small, tight-knit, predominantly white community. Instinct means I naturally gravitate towards other people of colour when I'm in a mainly white space; our shared Otherness makes me feel safer. I felt drawn in this way to a man at one of the first kink events I attended, and even considered striking up a conversation with him at a later date. Luckily, however, I was steered away from him by more experienced members of the scene who noticed he had a tendency to approach young women who were new to kink to tie, and would do so above either of their skill levels. They'd also watched him tie previously and considered him dangerous – in one incident, his model was in severe distress and he refused to take her down by cutting his rope (arguably, the fastest way to release someone). Later, I watched him deny these allegations by crying 'racism' instead of reflecting on and changing his behaviour. I have no doubt racism exists within the kink scene, but using this as an excuse to mask predatory behaviour makes it worse for everyone overall.

In the kink world, the term for a space where BDSM-related activities occur is a 'scene'. These are usually – though not always – planned in advance, and they don't necessarily involve sex or any sort of sexual activity. Generally speaking, in any given scene between two people, one is the top and one is the bottom. These terms aren't directly related to physical positions, and someone who likes to both top and bottom will usually identify as a 'switch'.

I used to see myself as strictly a bottom and a submissive, but I have been nudging towards switching. It's something I've been trying, and I'm finding it more enjoyable than I thought I would. But I still definitely have a more submissive mindset when I'm fucking. It's a headspace I slip into almost involuntarily. I can snap back to my usual self at the drop of a hat, which can sometimes be jarring for the people I play with – I've often been heard cackling at a joke mere seconds after the end of an intense scene. I've also never really experienced 'sub space', a phenomenon where a submissive feels floaty and spacey after a scene.

I like fucking – or rather, being fucked – especially when there's pain involved. But even after a decade and counting of enjoying this, I still feel slightly uncomfortable about it – why do I need the pain and the adrenaline that comes from being hurt? Does it mean I'm broken in some way? This idea seems to be quite common. Numerous threads on Quora, an open public forum, follow this line of thinking, with questions like: *Are people often into BDSM because of a past trauma?; Why do I enjoy watching BDSM, tied up, degraded, etc., but I'd never personally want it? If I like this and normal vanilla sex bores me, is that bad?; Do weird sexual fetishes stem from childhood or more specifically childhood trauma?*

And even though I know I'm not *broken*, even though studies have shown no evidence for 'BDSM being a maladaptive coping mechanism in response to early life dynamics',[3] I think about it more often than I'd like. I wonder if there was something small and seemingly inconsequential that happened during my childhood to lead me down this path, a ripple effect that's pushed me towards whips and rope and pain. I'm happy to have found the kink scene and, with it, people who share the same joys and doubts as me – but like that tightly bound knot of shame I used to feel after having sex, it is something I still struggle to resolve and reconcile, a barnacle of doubt clinging to the back of my brain.

Contrary to popular belief, liking rough sex doesn't give men permission to treat me however they want in bed. Some men assume it means I'm up for anything, that consent is all but moot because I like it rough. While I'm usually willing and able to do a lot, there are certain things and positions I like more than others – which would almost certainly make the sex better (and hotter), if only they'd stop for a second to ask and listen.

I once slept with a guy whose idea of dirty talk involved gratuitous descriptions of rape, and even though the sex was consensual, I was so shocked at his words that my brain froze and I couldn't think of anything to say in response while it was happening. It was only after he'd left that I had time and space to properly process what had happened. I'm lucky to have never been sexually assaulted, but what if I had? What if this sort of dirty talk triggered traumatic memories? Is this how he treats any woman who discloses their kinks to him?

I thought about messaging him – maybe a polite message, calmly explaining why what he had done was inappropriate, and asking him to reconsider his behaviour the next time he's in a similar situation; maybe an angry message, hoping to instil the fear of god into him so another woman wouldn't have to be subject to his behaviour. But I did neither. He wasn't worth my time and energy, and that's assuming he'd be willing to have a considered conversation about it in the first place.

I'd actually forgotten all about this incident until we rematched on a dating app. He mentioned we'd fucked before, and that he'd be keen to see me again. I honestly didn't even remember him until he asked me if I still liked it rough, and if I still lived in the same apartment. When I realised it was that guy, I told him our previous encounter had made me feel uncomfortable.

It's just fantasy though, he replied. *It's not real, obviously it's not real – can't you tell the difference between real life and fantasy?*

I didn't know how to reply.

The first kink event I attended in person was a casual rope session. It was in a discreet location, a warehouse in an inner-city Brisbane suburb. I was nervous, even though I met a friend beforehand to get a drink before we walked there together. After signing in, a few introductions, and a tour of the venue, she settled into a conversation with her friends, and I was left to fend for myself.

There were separate spaces for chilling out and for play, a formula replicated in almost every other kink venue both nationally and internationally, although I didn't know it yet. The people who weren't playing were just chatting. Some conversations veered towards kink, but others wouldn't have been out of place in any other social setting: complaining about work, talking about dinner the previous night, airing frustrations about Australia Post being inconsistent and delivering parcels to the incorrect address.

I moved slowly around the space, and while I was watching a scene, I tried to make myself as small as possible, to disappear into the background. I found myself averting my eyes, as if being seen watching, even by those who wanted to be watched, was something I should be embarrassed about.

There are many different types of play, and that's even before you venture outside the world of rope. As a very quick introduction, one of the ways to classify rope play is through contact with the ground. Floor work is, as the name suggests, conducted on the floor. Suspensions are instances where the model is suspended above the ground to a hard point, which can be a piece of bamboo, a wooden crossbeam, or an anchor point drilled into the ceiling. Partial suspensions (my personal favourite) occur when part of the model's body remains on the ground; having my right leg tied to a point while I'm still standing on my left foot is an example of a partial.

I didn't know any of this terminology when I went to that

first event, but I was still fascinated as I watched a guy do a self-suspension (or a 'selfie', as I later learnt they were called) – this is a suspension where the model is also the rigger. I watched another woman do a self-suspension in a quieter area of the venue after asking someone to be her spotter, then I watched a man suspend a woman in a tough position called a 'scorpion'. At the end of the night, I watched another woman and her partner in a scene. He inverted her, then whipped her, with varying degrees of force.

After I got home, I was suddenly anxious and clammy, shaking ever so slightly. I felt like I was having a panic attack. I think I was too overwhelmed by what I had seen and experienced and felt, even though the event was only supposed to be a casual gathering. By watching those people, I couldn't help but feel like I had been invading their privacy, an uninvited voyeur – and some of the Christian guilt I thought I'd exorcised long ago had come back to haunt me.

For a few days afterwards, I wasn't sure if I wanted to go to another event. My partner, who I was only seeing casually at the time, had tied me a few times by then, and I was beginning to love the feeling of rope biting into my skin. In an attempt to assuage my fears about taking my kink into a more public sphere, I researched and read all the shibari- and bondage-related material I could get my hands on; there's a surprising amount of information out there if you're a nerd and like reading and want to be as prepared as possible for something that is, for all intents and purposes, dangerous – and potentially fatal.

Rope is risky; it's not uncommon for things to go wrong. Suspension is hard on the body, and you have a limited amount of time once you're off the ground. This time limit differs from person to person – even for the same person, day to day. Sometimes I can be in the air for ten minutes, other times only a few seconds. Even when you're on the ground, rope can cause nerve damage, both temporary and permanent; broken limbs; asphyxiation; and, in severe cases, death. I was told early on that nerve damage was the most common injury in rope circles, and this became increasingly apparent as I spent more time in the scene. I'm reminded of these initial warnings every time a friend tells me about a damaged nerve, every time I read a story about wrist drop – losing full function of one or both hands for six to twelve months – of numbness that lasts for weeks on end. People have died as a result of mismanaged rope; they've been rendered paraplegic because the length of rope holding them in the air snapped unexpectedly and they landed on their head or neck.

Personally, I've experienced numbness in my fingers and I've had numb patches on my collarbone and on sections of my thighs after scenes. A friend of mine has lost count of the number of times and places she's had something go numb. Nerves are fragile, and repeated pressure can make them friable. I've had to be cut out of rope; I've thrown up a mess of bacon and toast and scrambled eggs after a tough tie in the high humidity of Brisbane in January while wearing a 旗袍 made of stiff fabric that retains heat; I've fainted – if only briefly – because a piece of neck rope had pressed too hard on my carotid artery.

60

There are ways to manage this risk, though it's important to remember that such risk cannot be completely mitigated. I've learnt to do finger checks: touching each of your fingers to your thumb to make sure you still have mobility, even if the fingers feel numb. I've learnt to tell the top I'm playing with when my arms or fingers or toes start to tingle, when they go numb, how much longer I can last in a particular position, if and when I need to come down immediately, when something is making me uncomfortable.

I've learnt about protocols for scenes – not just what to do during them, in them, but how to act respectfully around others who may be playing near you. I've learnt about consent and negotiations, which may be extensive, depending on who you're with, and where. I've learnt that some people might ask for you to fill out questionnaires, some may negotiate online, others might insist on negotiating in person. My negotiation list is brief – I don't have any specific triggers or any major physical impediments. I might mention slight variations in my mood, or if I have a new tattoo, but otherwise, I'm good to go.

Learning about kink didn't just expand my sexual horizons – a good scene is all about good communication. I've had to call a scene prematurely because something didn't feel right or my body just couldn't sustain the tie on that particular day. I'm pretty good at recognising when things aren't right, and my partner likes to be able to tell how I'm feeling by the sounds I make while I'm in the air. I always feel bad when I have to call a scene, even if it was the right thing to do. I feel like I'm not tough enough, that I've failed in some intangible way, that I've messed up the scene not only for me, but also for the other person or people involved.

That being said, I've had plenty of amazing experiences during my time in the kink scene. I've had two of my girl friends tie me up and beat me until I had bruises running up and down my thighs; I've had a rigger use a carabiner to pry my mouth open; I've had needles threaded through the skin on my back; I've had bottle caps pressed into my shins, creating scars that took weeks to fade; and much more. Kink has made me happier, stronger, and bolder. I've learnt more about my needs and desires as they pertain to sex, and how to communicate these clearly and without reservation – something that has also strengthened the way I communicate in my relationships and in my life in general.

Most of the faces at that first kink event, as well as many of the parties and events I've been to since, whether they be in Adelaide or Perth or Sydney, were white. Every time I enter a room, especially if it's a room full of people I've never met before, I scan for a number of visibly non-white people, then the number of women. It's almost an instinct of mine nowadays. The Melbourne scene is more racially diverse than the Brisbane scene, but that could be chalked up to the fact that Melbourne has a more diverse population.

This lack of diversity is magnified by an incident at my first visit to a kink venue in Melbourne: an older man, probably in his fifties, sidled up to me and asked me what I was into. I ran through an abridged version of my list, and he stopped me halfway through to ask if I'd ever been interested in race play. I started to say no, but before I knew it, he'd launched into an intense description of how he was into Japanese internment camp style play. I was too stunned to reply properly, so I muttered something like 'I'm not Japanese,' excused myself from the conversation, and made a mental note to avoid him for the rest of the night.

It's something of an unspoken rule that kink venues and events have a zero-tolerance policy on homophobia, transphobia, misogyny, and overt racism, but things can get murkier when it comes to the realm of 'fantasy'. I told my partner about this incident, but I didn't tell anyone at the venue. I didn't want to make a fuss, especially because it was unlikely I'd ever see that man again. Maybe I should have said something, just in case this man ended up saying something similar to someone newer to the scene, and maybe I would have, if this had occurred in Brisbane.

Reflecting on it now, maybe I also wasn't sure if I would be taken seriously – perhaps it would be waved off as a matter of 'preference'. This incident, and the fact that I'm still thinking about it years after it happened, serves as a continual and bleak reminder of how far some so-called progressive communities still have to go. The scene is queer friendly and extremely accepting of neurodiversity, but can be squeamish about tackling issues of race head-on. People acknowledge the need for and practise enthusiastic consent, but it is still a place where young people can fall victim to sexual predators under the guise of an unhealthy and poorly negotiated dynamic.

I messaged a friend a few months after the incident in Melbourne, and I mentioned I simply feel safer when I'm around other people of colour.

'Is it like being the only woman in a room full of men?' she asked.

'Similar,' I said, trying to think of the right words to describe the feelings of unease and unbelonging. 'It's more subtle, though, in the way that the power of white privilege is more subtle than the visible physical power of men.'

'Ah yeah, that makes sense,' she replied, and I breathed a sigh of relief. She's a queer woman, so she knows a little about what it's like to be on the margins – but she's still a white woman and, historically, white women don't have the best track record when it comes to issues around race.

I have a separate, private Instagram for my kink photos, and the photos I post are meticulously curated and edited so my face (and nipples, which are apparently not allowed on Instagram despite male nipples being fine) cannot be seen by the wider public. I know I'd have more followers if my account was public, but I am grateful for the extra layer of security the 'private' account gives me when I have to fend off random dudes who aren't connected to any sort of scene at all, or when I have the power to simply reject a follow request from *a MALE,*

& a lover of bondage, erotica, feet, etc whose profile name is 'asianfeet1963'. Aside from the general grossness of the internet, I find it's a great way to meet others – specifically, other Asian women – who are also interested in kink.

The people I follow on this account are located all over the world, and one lazy Sunday evening, I started a conversation with a Chinese American woman about rope and her local scene. On Instagram, her photos show her beaming while tied to a piece of bamboo, her face unmarred by blur or filter. In other photos, she is mid-scene, her face and body contorted. These photos are also untouched, and even though I am aware of the facade that is social media, I couldn't help but think to myself, *She seems so carefree.*

She told me her community was also predominantly white, but she doesn't let it bother her too much. I wish I had her confidence. I have a special admiration for this woman.

I began to wonder if I was the problem; if I'd just stop thinking about race all the time, then maybe I'd be more chill about everything. I talked to a wide range of people in the Brisbane kink community about its overwhelming whiteness, and during these conversations some asked me exactly this – why do I care about this so much? – a question that could only come from someone who hasn't spent their whole life thinking about the effect of race on their everyday lives. Is it so unusual that I'd want to feel comfortable in the spaces I frequent – especially if I'm going to be half-naked, with my safety and life in someone else's hands?

Another reason I'm given for the dearth of non-white faces

is the stigma attached to kink and sexual openness that is common throughout communities of colour. In my experience, Chinese people are more likely to hold conservative values and are reluctant to talk about sex at all, so it would make sense for this to extend to disdain for anything kink-related.

It's part of the reason I try to keep these parts of my life separate. I'm not ashamed of my kinky side, but I know how the internet works and how easy it is to take a screenshot and forward it on, and I'm not sure what excuse I would use if my parents saw photos of me in my underwear, dangling from the ceiling. I could try and pre-empt this by explaining the kink scene to them, but I know that conversation wouldn't end well – yet another weight to the crippling burden of secrets I keep from them, for both their sanity and mine. However, I'm not sure this is a phenomenon unique to communities of colour. Many of my white friends also blur or obscure their faces on their kink-related Instagram photos and don't talk about this part of their life with their families.

I don't know what the right answer is here – I don't think there even is a right answer. I want to see more non-white faces in the kink community, but I also don't want to force people out of their comfort zones for my sake or benefit. Maybe there are people like me out there who are interested in kink but prefer to indulge themselves in the privacy of their own bedrooms, or maybe they simply don't know who to talk to or where to go to get started. I know how tricky it can be, especially if you don't know anyone who's already in the scene and involved in these sorts of events.

My kink Instagram almost exclusively features rope bondage – of me being tied, and, to a lesser extent, me tying. There are two kinds of bondage in the kink scene: Western(-inspired) bondage; and Japanese(-inspired) bondage, or kinbaku/shibari (the terms are, for all intents and purposes, interchangeable). The latter is derived from 捕縄術 (hojojutsu), the use of rope by Japanese warrior nobles to restrain and torture prisoners, allowing them to 'be tied to a fixed support or even suspended from the ceiling of a prison'.[4] (Of personal interest to me is the fact that the idea of using rope for military purposes was known as 綿縄套索 and Chinese in origin.) Hojojutsu was adopted by Japanese city police before modern forms of restraint rendered it obsolete, and elements of it still remain in traditional Japanese martial arts. Another part of Japanese society, however, took inspiration from it and honed it into what is now commonly known as kinbaku, separated into a few different lineages, each with their own respective masters.

Even before I attended that first rope event, I was aware I'd be stepping into a community of mainly white people practising an art derived from and heavily steeped in Japanese culture. This added to my apprehension around joining the kink scene – I knew I liked being tied up, but I also knew I wouldn't want to be part of anything that seemed even slightly disrespectful. I know all too well what it's like to have ideas and symbols I hold dear misappropriated by the West.

I've attended a variety of classes, all as a rope bottom (the person being tied), and every shibari class I've been to in

Australia has been taught by white people – albeit white people who have lived in Japan for a while or studied under specific Japanese 緊縛し (shibari masters). The first class I went to took place on a crisp Tuesday night in a specially designed studio in Brisbane's southern suburbs. The ceiling was crisscrossed with sturdy wooden beams, and the mats were slightly springy beneath my bare feet. This was a beginner's class, so the teacher went through the basics before demonstrating a pattern, step by step. The students followed. Others who had already learnt the pattern practised under supervision – tie, adjust, untie, rest. Rinse, repeat.

Most of the classes I attended after this followed a similar structure. All in all, I was pleasantly surprised at the degree of respect afforded to Japan and the Japanese at large by most shibari practitioners (to be fair, my bar had been set pretty low) – except for their attitudes towards tying in Japanese traditional dress.

On Instagram, if you know where to look, it is easy to find photos of gorgeous Japanese models being tied while draped in kimonos, and there are some (white people, mainly) who want to emulate this look, and who argue that by tying in a kimono they are simply trying to respect and 'show off' their love for Japanese culture. I am vehemently opposed to this opinion, but I don't feel safe enough in this community of mainly white people to speak up. Wearing a kimono in Japan is different from wearing a kimono in Australia, just like wearing a qipao in China is different from wearing a qipao in Australia. Cultural context matters, and it's not for white people to decide when it should be taken into account during such discussions. I have only once worn a kimono for a scene, and it was under very specific terms: I had been invited to do so by a Japanese person in Japan. I would feel extremely uncomfortable doing so under any other circumstances.

It wasn't long after all these firsts that I went to Japan with my partner for a part-holiday part-kinbaku study tour – we saw four different 緊縛し in the space of about twelve days. I was still relatively new to kink and rope and shibari, so I saw it as a learning opportunity as much as anything else.

We tied in tiny rope bars in Shinjuku and Osaka. They were vibrant, warm, welcoming venues hidden behind plain white doors adorned only with their respective unit numbers, in basements and in buildings where a rickety lift was just big enough for two people. Thick pieces of bamboo dangled above our heads, courtesy of wooden beams or hard points that had been drilled into the ceiling. There were drinks, alcoholic and otherwise, genuine attempts at conversation through broken English and Japanese and via translation apps, and, of course, people tying.

I savoured the sound of uncoiling jute on tatami – gentle thwacks that varied in intensity depending on how fast the rope was travelling through the rigger's hands. These were punctuation marks in the conversations I was having with my partner, a quiet juxtaposition to the feeling of being bound and restrained. I began to understand what it meant to generate and sustain a connection through a tie. I was humbled by the generosity of our Japanese hosts, and the openness with which they talked about sex.

We visited bookshops and corner stores where whole aisles were filled with manga, many of them emblazoned with smiling drawings of young women with truly enormous boobs. Sometimes they were covered, but more often than not they were nearly falling out of their tops. I worried about these fantastical girls' backs and wondered if they would grow up to have back problems, but I also marvelled at the fact that these images weren't censored for children. We went to a cotton-candy pink, six-storey sex shop in the middle of Akihabara, which sold everything from vibrator earrings to skimpy lingerie and sex toys, and we skulked around nondescript laneways until we found a fetish shop filled with shelves upon shelves of DVDs and magazines and BDSM paraphernalia.

We attended a rope performance in a space that seemed like it should have only accommodated about twenty or so people, but by the time the doors closed, there would have been at least fifty people crammed in that small room. The event went for four or five hours, far longer than we expected, and afterwards my neck was tired from constantly craning to see the stage. Of course, it was emceed in Japanese, and my partner was one of only two conspicuously foreign attendees. I was also, obviously, a foreign attendee, but despite not being Japanese, I felt strangely comfortable. It was the first time I had been to a kink event where non-white faces outnumbered white ones.

*

It was only after the trip to Japan that I fully understood what people meant when they talked about kink as a form of connection. It sounds wishy-washy, but I began to see each scene as a conversation, a moment to *be* with the person I'm playing with. The scene doesn't have to be complicated or difficult in any way for it to have meaning; conversely, the trickiest scene in the world could fall flat if each person is simply going through the motions instead of engaging with the feelings at hand.

My partner and I talk about subtleties between surrender and resistance or tolerance – that sometimes more is made of the ability to sustain a tie as opposed to what happens between the people engaged in the scene itself. It's a fine line to toe: I don't want my surrender to be taken as weakness, for tops to think I can't handle pain, but an act of surrender is also an act of trust, especially when that person is about to put you up in the air.

About six months after our trip to Japan, my partner and I tied in a club in Melbourne. It was a different environment, different people, different atmosphere. We barely knew anyone there, which was a nice change. It was dark, but there were coloured lights in every corner, flashing white and red and blue and green. They gave off a cool yet edgy vibe, and it was just enough to be able to see what was going on. There were booths nestled around the edge of the venue – spaces to sit and chat, or for more private play, if the mood should strike. When we arrived, there was a woman being tied to a cage by another woman, latex-clad; there was a young man being flogged while his hands and feet were locked into stocks. There were more people there than at any event I'd been to in Brisbane. The music was louder, the space was bigger, and there was more alcohol.

The only rigging frame available was located on the stage. I have stage fright, and I knew people would be watching, but I felt calm. The floor was cold and *I* was cold because it was Melbourne and it was winter – and then my partner wrapped his arms around me, I closed my eyes, he started laying rope across my body, and everything began to fall away.

I can't remember the specifics of our scene, but I remember how I felt: I didn't feel like I was performing, even though we were literally on stage. I don't know what I looked like or what shapes I made because no-one took any photos.

Afterwards, we went upstairs for a drink. It was brighter there, but just as loud. I was watching a man spank a woman who had been tied to an internal railing when another woman approached us and asked about our scene. She asked about the pain – whether or not it hurt and how much it hurt – and I found it difficult to articulate my answer. 'It hurts … but it doesn't?' I fumbled. I felt uncomfortably self-aware.

'You looked like you were meditating,' she said, more than once. Her turn of phrase gave me pause. I'd never thought of scenes in that way, but she's right. I always close my eyes because I want to be in the moment, not worrying about the lights and colours and movements of people around me. I consciously focus on relaxing, and it makes space for my mind to slow down enough to think about one or two things instead of the usual six or eight. I hold a lot of tension in my shoulders and upper back, and it's a chance for me to focus on relaxing those muscles.

In a scene, there are no expectations other than the ones I put on myself. I'm in control of the situation. I'm able to just *be*.

I can't remember exactly when I bought my first set of rope, but it would have been a couple of years after I was introduced to it; I was curious about self-tying. It hung off a curtain rod, untouched for a month or two, while I attended to life and work and writing. But eventually, I was drawn back to it, and slowly, with the help of the internet and some friends, I picked up a few simple patterns.

I learnt that tying a pattern, whether it be on myself or someone else, is easy. Even tying a pattern *well* is easy, with enough practice. It's just rote learning combined with muscle memory – if I close my eyes, I can visualise the pattern being tied right in front of me. What's difficult is everything else – the intangibles, the ability to start and sustain a conversation with a piece of rope. It's something that can only be gained through time and practice, and I know I am lucky to have the luxury to do so.

I find self-tying almost relaxing – there's something therapeutic about the feel and flow of rope through my hands before it tightens against my skin, and the ability to manage my own release. At the same time, it requires more focus than it first seems. You take on the responsibilities of top and bottom when you self-tie, and it's a lot to keep track of even if you have a spotter. Self-suspension brings with it another layer of risk – you don't just need to make sure you go up without hurting yourself, but you need to remember to reserve some energy to get yourself down safely.

Every time I tie myself or am tied, I learn something new; kink in general has taught me to appreciate my body in new ways, through experiences that are uniquely kink-specific – it's hard not to feel just a little bit invincible after you've spent ten or so minutes dangling from the ceiling. It's also allowed me to experience platonic and sexual intimacy on so many different levels, and provided me with the space to make brilliant friendships with people I wouldn't have otherwise met. I've re-examined my sexuality with more care, and come to new conclusions for old questions.

I still worry about the stigma attached to kink and BDSM. Even though I know that being a feminist means I have agency over my body and I shouldn't feel ashamed for the things I want to do (or want other people to do to me), it somehow still feels incongruous with the fact that I like being choked out or slapped in the face or being spanked while draped over someone's knee.

But maybe that's why self-tying feels so different – and, ironically, freeing. Sometimes, all I need is barely a minute's worth of hanging upside down from a single line to feel the sting on my waist, and the blood rush to my head. In those moments, I feel something approximating relief; I feel more myself than I can ever imagine being when I'm on the ground.

her

她

4

Monsters

My childhood home is eerily quiet. It's not just because my parents live in a house that's too big for them, or because my room and my sister's have been left untouched for at least half a decade. It's always been too big a house for a family of four – one too many bedrooms, one too many bathrooms, one too many dining areas. Maybe that's why it's always been a house full of silences.

Some of these silences were self-imposed, others governed by unspoken rules. It was a place of bubbling anger and quiet resentment, of emotions either too big or too small to express; now it feels like a site of mild but repeating trauma that probably won't ever truly subside. It is a place of assumptions and absolute obedience – a place where the past is framed in smiling family photos and amusing anecdotes. Even now, my parents still joke about the fact that one of the two phrases my sister knows how to say in Fuchow, their dialect, is 'Hit on the bottom'.

Years after I moved out of home, I stayed in my old room overnight – I had an overseas flight leaving early in the morning from Coolangatta airport, and my dad had offered to drive me there. Being in the same single bed with the same teddy bear patchwork covers and the same faux woodgrain IKEA chest of drawers triggered a flood of upsetting memories. That evening, after dinner and an obligatory episode of *MasterChef*, I sobbed quietly into my pillow, just like I had done many times before as a kid. I woke up the next morning ridden with anxiety and an urge to leave the house as quickly as possible; it's been seven years now, and I haven't set foot in my old room since.

My parents' house looks like any other on their street – tiled roof, brick walls, a double garage, big palm trees in the front yard – but to me, it's a symbol of constraint and control. I've spent so long hiding in the shadows of what my parents expect me to say and do and think, especially when I'm in their presence, that it can be hard to do anything else. It's even harder to explain why my anxiety froths to the surface when my mother sends me a text out of the blue, even if it is just about the latest episode of *MasterChef*. I think it's because I'm afraid it will spiral into something more, or that it's a gentle precursor for the actual issue at hand. Her barbs are sharp and can come out of nowhere – there have been too many times when a seemingly innocuous conversation about the weather has turned abruptly into 'So what *are* you doing with your money now anyway?'

This ubiquitous feeling of entrapment is probably why I felt inexorably drawn to Gothic narratives while I was in high school, a feeling amplified upon my first reading of Edgar Allan Poe's short story *The Fall of the House of Usher*. My fascination with the Gothic continued well beyond year eleven English, though I wasn't a big fan of vampires and werewolves (keep in mind this was during the era of the *Twilight* craze). I took a Gothic literature course at university, and the Gothic eventually became an integral part of my honours thesis. Originally, I'd thought my interest in it sprang from its flexibility, its ability to reflect the anxieties of any particular time or place. Then I thought it was because of its links to postcolonial narratives and the ways in which writers have used Gothic conventions to critique and subvert the nation-state and everything it suppresses in order to survive.

Now I realise it might be because I grew up in a house that was too big for four people, a space where I wasn't allowed much agency, an environment where saving face came at the expense of genuine emotional engagement. M felt this too, though he didn't have the right words to express it at the time. I brought him over once, when my parents were overseas. 'It feels … empty,' he said, as I showed him around. 'Not physically empty, really, but just – I don't know – bare?'

It sounds dramatic to say I lived a Gothic childhood, or even a childhood infused with Gothic elements, but that's just it, isn't it? The Gothic thrives in pockets of seeming normality: the uncanny, hiding in plain sight.

Gothic narratives usually feature a big structure of some kind – a house, a church, a nunnery – that is a metonym for its inhabitants. The physicality of the structure usually reflects the psyche of the family: often broken in some way, despite outward appearances. This is eerily similar to the concept of 臉, a culturally enforced veneer of perfection not unlike something out of *The Stepford Wives*. I wasn't allowed to close my bedroom door at night, but I still felt claustrophobic, like I was always being watched, like I always had to put on my best face even when all I wanted to do was burst into tears.

I didn't just grow up in a Gothic house, in a Gothic environment, but also as the spitting image of and in the shadow of my mother. This manifested itself physically, as well as mentally and emotionally.

Like many others of their generation, my parents keep albums upon albums of photos. It's a physical version of Instagram, with captions hastily scrawled on the back of photo paper and a sepia tone that doesn't need to be applied via digital filter. There are photos of them with their classmates from primary school and high school, mostly arranged in chronological order. The albums they're in are also slowly falling apart; the plastic cracks a little more under my hands every time I gingerly flip from one page to another.

I once found a photo of my mother as a young woman while

I was trying to find photos of myself as a child. I was struck by how similar we looked – the structure and shape of our faces, the positioning of our hair and our facial features. I wondered what a colourised version of the photo would look like. When I mentioned this to my mother, she brushed it off. 'Out of the two of you, you were always the one who looked more like me,' she said.

In *Écrits: A Selection*, French psychoanalyist and psychiatrist Jacques Lacan proposed that all children pass through a stage of development where they learn to recognise themselves in their own reflection. He called it the mirror stage, and argued that it 'illustrates the conflictual nature of the dual relationship':[1] that is, the relationship between the person you are and the person you see when you look in the mirror. But what happens when you look in the mirror and you see your mother? Or, what happens if you look at your mother and you see yourself? Sometimes it's hard for me to rationalise and separate the attributes I share with my mother. I know nature and nurture play their separate roles, and I wonder how differently I would have turned out if my parents hadn't moved to Australia. I wonder how much more alike Mum and I would be if we hadn't been nudged in different directions at pivotal moments in our lives.

Mum and I even looked alike as babies – I once thought a photo of her as a baby was in fact a photo of me. 'Don't be ridiculous,' she berated, her face twisted in a strange combination of amusement and indignation. I wonder how alike she was to her mother – if she even had photos of her mother as a child to make those comparisons. Sometimes, when I look in the mirror, I can see my mother under my red hair and tortoiseshell glasses.

Classically, the doppelgänger* has been used to tease apart aspects of the human psyche and to explore the duality of human nature. In Edgar Allan Poe's short story *William Wilson*, the eponymous William is extremely disturbed by the presence of another William Wilson, the original William's conscience, who tries to guide him away from his amoral tendencies. At the end of this story, William kills his double, only to realise that by doing so, he has also killed himself.

However, as Milica Živković, an academic in the Faculty of Philosophy at the University of Niš, notes, the doppelgänger has also been used to reflect dualities between shadows, sisters, twins, lovers, and more.² Toni Morrison's novel *Sula* (Knopf, 1973) is a classic example. It is filled with doppelgängers – whether it be protagonists and best friends Sula Peace and Nel Wright, who not only do everything together as young girls, but also watch two people die without attempting to interfere; Nel and her mother, Helene, conventional wives and mothers who stay in their insular community; or Sula and her mother, Hannah, carefree spirits who have multiple affairs.

The doppelgänger is a trope that has morphed and endured – after all, there will always be something unsettling about someone who looks like you, let alone someone who looks and thinks like you. Mum and I aren't doppelgängers – at least, not in a conventional Gothic sense – but we share striking

---

* A double, look-alike, or alter-ego.

similarities. These similarities aren't just skin deep – and perhaps it is this that lies at the heart of our often-fractured relationship, what led us to see each other as adversaries as opposed to friends.

Mothers and daughters are destined to clash, but when I was a child or a young adult, our run-ins with each other weren't like the ones I saw on television or in movies, or even like the ones I saw between my friends and their mothers. Mum and I are both headstrong, hyper-focused, and refuse to yield unless absolutely necessary. Our clashes were never loud but they were still venomous, barbs traded through glances, a roll of the eyes, or malicious compliance. I also resented the level of power she held over me, the strength of that power, and the way in which she wielded it. It felt like she refused to grant me any of my requests just because she *could*, even in the face of what I thought were perfectly logical and sound reasons – I was grounded for six weeks when I was nineteen because I dared to stay over at a friend's house. I may have projected an image of stoicism and obedience, but I think she always knew there was more than I let on, that there was a simmering resentment under my seemingly calm veneer.

'I regret teaching you girls to be independent,' she said to me once, in English. I can't remember what the conversation was about, but I will never forget that line. I was in my early to mid teens, and when I heard those words, I felt I'd been stabbed in the gut. My mum is one of the most independent women I know – she left her family behind when she came to Australia to study on her own, again when she went to work in Singapore, and once more when she migrated to Australia to raise a family. She has run a single-woman business for over twenty years, and she's still going strong.

My perception of Mum changed after this moment. Part of me rendered her vindictive and monstrous – I was a teenager in that stage of anti-parent rebellion, and it was easier to think of her as a one-dimensional character because I knew we'd never have a serious conversation about what she really meant by that statement. I think I now understand what she was trying to say – that it's difficult for parents to let go of their children, to set them free into a world they've worked so hard to protect them from and against. I also acknowledge I won't really know what it's like to be a mother until I have a child of my own – which means I won't know the emotions associated with caring for and loving someone before letting them go into a world fraught with danger and possibility, letting them fend for themselves. I acknowledge this, but I don't think I will ever be able to truly forgive her for saying those words out loud.

The silent war between headstrong Chinese mother and daughter is exemplified in the film *Everything Everywhere All at Once* (A24, 2022). In the film, Michelle Yeoh's character, Evelyn, has a fractious relationship with her daughter, Joy – in this universe, the Alpha-Verse, and presumably many of the other parallel universes mentioned throughout. The first time I watched it, I was on my own in a pitch-black South Bank cinema, tears periodically streaming down my face, staining my glasses, and dampening my sleeves.

It wasn't just the blend of Mandarin, Chinese, and English in the film that made me emotional, but also the depiction and progression of the relationship between mother and daughter. Evelyn's parenting style frustrates Joy, and it is her willingness to push her daughter that turns the Alpha-Verse version of Joy into Jobu Tupaki, the villain of the film. They're the only people able to experience the simultaneity of all the universes at once, and we're led to believe that Jobu Tupaki is trying to kill Evelyn until they meet and she reveals that she was just looking for someone who could relate to her, someone who knew what it was like to be burdened with the things she could see and feel.

Sadly, the desire for such a connection isn't enough to make it so, and in the film this revelation doesn't immediately change the tenor of their relationship. I think Mum wants to have a stronger connection with me, to know more about my life, and I want to know more about hers, but our stubbornness means we've ended up in a strange stalemate that neither of us feels like we can break, for fear of emotional vulnerability with no meaningful return. Even though we're on more solid ground nowadays, an unspoken hurt lines the tension between us, which is why it feels like Joy from *Everything Everywhere All at Once* is in my head when she tells her mother that they somehow always end up hurting each other when they're together, when she gently asks her mother to let her go.

I'm sure my relationship with my mother would be much worse if I hadn't moved out of home when I did. Mum didn't let me go as much as I wrenched myself free, and I wonder how different our lives and our relationship would be in alternate universes, how different it could have been in this one – a fruitless endeavour, but one I engage in nonetheless. What if it could have all turned on something said or withheld? What would those people be like? I wonder if Mum thinks about this too – I know she's aware of the tension between us, but her attempts to deal with this manifest themselves in the rewriting of our collective memories, in the construction of alternate realities.

I have a memory of Mum talking to my sister and me when we were both in our late teens and still living at home. As we set the table for dinner, she relayed a story about a few of her patients forcing their children to study specific subjects in their final years of high school. 'You're lucky, you know,' she said, raising her eyebrows. 'We're not like those other parents – we let you choose what you wanted to do.' I remember watching her pacing the length of the kitchen and dining area, my eyes raising to meet her general shape but deliberately avoiding eye contact.

She was – as always – technically correct, but I was put under immense pressure to pick physics instead of music in year eleven, which meant two years of classes in something I wasn't great at and didn't really like. Later, I also felt pressured to list medicine as my top preference for university, even though I had no intention of following through on a medical degree. She paid for me to attend training courses for the medical admissions exam and to sit the exam itself, despite my objections and with the full knowledge that I didn't want to study medicine. That evening, when she told us we were lucky, the term 'gaslighting' wasn't in as frequent circulation or as well understood as it is now, but I knew her words had made me uncomfortable for a reason.

I think Mum still believes her version of events is true, and I know memory is a tricky thing. We are all unreliable narrators of our own stories, picking and choosing scenes and rewriting them over and over in our minds until we have convinced ourselves of the truth. This is, after all, how myths are formed – even the small ones we tell ourselves.

My parents aren't bad people. My sister and I always had enough to eat, we had great educations, we were given almost all the opportunities we wanted – and even some we didn't want. I believe, wholeheartedly, that they thought they were doing what was best for us. Like all humans, they are nuanced, with their own experiences and biases. But to this day, I still struggle to accept their approach to punishment.

When we were children, my sister and I were caned with strips of bamboo. At the time, I didn't know how my parents acquired them or how they kept getting fresh ones, but thanks to my foray into indoor plants and my burgeoning obsession with growing my own vegetables as an adult, I'm now fairly certain they sourced them from the gardening section at Bunnings. In any case, the ones in use were stored next to the bread and the fruit bowl in an alcove beside the pantry. They were about a metre long, skinny – as thick as a HB pencil – a light tan in colour, with dark-brown bands encircling them intermittently. One end was tied off in a looped twist that looked like a Q – this was the end that would be gripped in calm, white-knuckled fury. The other end was for inflicting punishment.

The fresh canes were tied up neatly with a rubber band and lived on the top shelf in my parents' walk-in wardrobe. Each one began straight, but after a few uses, a slight bend would appear. It was preferable to be hit with a fresh cane, because the old ones would also fray, creating a cat-o'-nine-tails-like effect that allowed the split bamboo to generate what I can only describe as an aftershock.

When I talk about being caned, I don't mean a rap on the knuckles or a few light taps. The strokes were usually unleashed on my bottom, the number determined by a combination of the mood of the administering parent and the severity of my wrongdoing. Backchat meant one or two strokes, with more added if I was silly enough to keep going. Failing to finish my maths or Chinese homework could get me a few strokes, too. Banging around and carrying on in frustration – an imitation of my parents when they were angry – was another sure-fire way to earn five or ten strokes.

Being caned, like any sort of physical punishment, is an experience that triggers all five senses. There is the smell of fear, of knowing what is about to happen, knowing there is no escape. I often kept my eyes closed, but if I wasn't fast enough I would sometimes see a flash of light brown before I felt the cane strike my skin. There is the physical sting, a sharp pain that reverberates outward from the point of impact. This was always compounded by the next stroke, which came too quickly for any endorphins to have kicked in. And there is the sound of the cane – the thwack – with maybe a few smaller thwacks if the cane is split at the ends. There is the taste of blood in my mouth, the taste of tears as they roll down my cheeks and meet my lips. And then there is release – physical, emotional, and mental, all at once, but only after the allocated strokes have been delivered.

I have a relatively high pain threshold, which serves me well when it comes to masochism and kink, and I wonder if there's something of a symbiotic relationship here – that this pain tolerance is a result of being struck as a child. In any case, caning, which many in the kink scene enjoy, continues to and probably will always be one of my hard limits.

As a child, it didn't take long for me to see my parents as cane-wielding figures. I was small in age and size, and the cane made me small in spirit, too. I withered under their gaze, and all these years later, I still shrink in their presence. I rationalised it in my head at the time because that was the only way I could get through it – but even then, I wondered how this administering of corporal punishment fit with the religious beliefs they had impressed upon me; wasn't Christianity all about love and kindness and patience?

Christianity and Chinese culture have more in common than I'd like. They both espouse conservative values and the importance of community; I grew up calling anyone who is older than me 哥哥 or 姊姊, 阿姨 or 叔叔, just as we are brothers and sisters in Christ. There is also a strong emphasis on family. The first part of the fifth commandment, 'honour your father and mother', is '孝順父母' in Chinese. It seems relatively innocent, but 孝順 means more than just honour. It means honour, respect, and obedience, all rolled into one. It means you should be filial. It means family comes first, and you will be damned if you see it any other way.

Because this concept is so intangible and difficult to explain, it's rare to see any mention of it in any media, let alone any nuanced discussion. So when I read Weike Wang's novel *Chemistry* (Knopf, 2017), I immediately connected with the protagonist – a Chinese woman who quits her chemistry PhD without her parents' knowledge. She also refuses to accept a marriage proposal from her white boyfriend, Eric, who is often confused by her filial nature. She says:

> I don't want to get married until I have done more for myself. But I also owe it to them [her parents] to do more for myself, which is what Eric didn't understand; he said, You shouldn't owe them anything. We argue over this. The American brings up the individual. The Chinese brings up *xiao shun* [孝順]. When I ask Eric if he thinks a child can ever feel entirely independent of her parents, he says, What kind of question is that?[3]

It's a question I think about a lot, a question I don't think I'll ever be able to definitively answer. There's also a sense of melancholy in her words that resounds with me – this feeling that maybe I'm still not enough, that I haven't achieved enough for them. I love my parents, but the reason I don't see them very much these days is because this pressure becomes almost unbearable in person. I have come to resent the total obedience they demand of me, what I see as their over-reliance on God.

It's hard to reconcile their genuine love for my sister and me, their desire for us to do well in life, with the violent and almost heartless act of caning and their willingness to sweep away the consequences of such acts through a combination of jokes and silences.

As a child, I knew I couldn't tell anyone else about the caning, and over the years I have wrestled with an ingrained compulsion to maintain this self-imposed censorship – to save face on behalf of my family. There are still large silences and gaps in the conversation around this kind of domestic violence, especially when an interplay of cultural values is present, and I know there must be plenty of people who end up taking these sorts of secrets to the grave. The caning stopped when I was in my early teens, but this also coincided with an extended period of bullying at school. The trauma, and the accompanying feelings of utter loneliness and emptiness, I now realise, have never really disappeared.

Even though Dad was the one who administered most of the canings, we all knew Mum was the one calling the shots. I respect my mum, but even now, I am deeply afraid of her. I don't know how hearing this would make her feel – if she would be horrified, or if she would simply accept it as the natural way of Chinese families. There have been times, especially during my teenage years, where I have been quick to pass judgement on her and her decisions: not allowing me to go to friends' houses for parties or sleepovers, pushing me to go to North Shore and James An scholarship classes, forcing my hair into a bowl cut even though all I wanted was to tie it into a ponytail like the other girls at school.

As I've grown older, I've become increasingly torn between recognising that she was trying to do her best – or at least, what she thought was best at the time – and that her controlling behaviour meant I couldn't just *enjoy* being a kid. It's important for me to remember that she is a nuanced human being with her own experiences and biases, and her actions and decisions were born from her upbringing and cultural heritage. That being said, many of her rules when I was growing up matched those set by Amy Chua, of *Battle Hymn of the Tiger Mother* (Penguin Random House, 2011) fame.

The release of Chua's book in 2011 coincided with my first year of university. It stirred up discussion and controversy – mainly online, and mainly in America, where Chua and her family live – for many reasons, least of all for Chua's pride in and defence of her parenting methods. This was a time when I was still grappling with teenagehood and what it meant to be a Malaysian Chinese teenager in Australia. Mum tried to maintain her control over my life, but I had a university schedule that included lectures at eight in the morning and labs that didn't finish until five in the evening, which meant I could stretch the truth as to my whereabouts without raising too much suspicion. This allowed for a veneer of freedom I'd never experienced before – something I savoured and clung to as if it could all disappear overnight. I didn't feel like Mum was as extreme as Chua, but some of her rules were similar to those Chua imposed on her daughters: we weren't allowed sleepovers, we very rarely had play dates, and we were expected to get As (though this loosened slightly during high school) and practise our chosen musical instruments for at least an hour a day.

My mum, like many Asian mums, is tough. She's hard on herself, too, and that transfers into the way she parents. It's a trait many immigrant mothers share – an inheritance of hard work and resilience they feel compelled to instil in their own children. When I was younger, I saw her as something of a tyrant. She was the queen of our household, and what she said was normally the way things turned out. Now my sister and I are living out of home, she's softened a little, but childhood habits die hard, and I still see her as the strict, steely-eyed head of our family.

I am slightly uncomfortable about characterising my mother in this way. I know I should respect my parents – the legacy of 孝順父母 looms large – and I don't want to contribute to the overarching narrative of the overbearing 'Asian parent'. But this seems irreconcilable with my memories of her ignoring me when I tried to speak up for myself, the pressure I felt from her to succeed at school and in my musical endeavours, and her expectations for me to be the perfect Chinese Christian girl.

The two most popular stereotypes of East Asian women in popular culture are the delicate and beautiful 'Oriental flower' and the monstrous and fierce 'dragon lady'. As Joey Lee, a former contributor to and now editor of Wilfrid Laurier University's undergraduate academic journal *Bridges*, notes, Hollywood popularised these two archetypes to establish British and American imperial dominance, exploit society's views on the so-called 'Yellow Peril', and 'to develop a culture of paranoid xenophobia'.[4]

The dragon lady stereotype isn't as widespread as the Oriental flower, but it is common enough for it to be a staple in popular culture, and it is just as damaging – see O-Ren Ishii (Lucy Liu) in *Kill Bill* (A Band Apart, 2003), or Eleanor Sung-Young (Michelle Yeoh), the domineering matriarch in *Crazy Rich Asians* (SK Global, 2018). This stereotype isn't new – in 1933, Anna May Wong, who is considered by many to be Hollywood's first Chinese American star, was interviewed for *Film Weekly* in an article that was eventually published under the headline 'I Protest'. In this conversation, which took place nearly a century ago, she asks, 'Why is it that the screen Chinese is nearly always the villain? And so crude a villain. Murderous, treacherous, a snake in the grass. We are not like that.'[5]

This trope is a form of Othering, a way for Western society

to see itself as superior to those 'foreigners' on the basis of civility. The Other, we must not forget, is to be feared. In his seminal work, *Orientalism*,* Edward Said, a Palestinian American professor of literature and accomplished literary critic, notes that 'standardisation and cultural stereotyping have intensified the hold of the nineteenth-century academic and imaginative demonology of the "mysterious Orient"',[6] a phenomenon that has continued throughout the twentieth and twenty-first centuries. Said's specific choice of the term 'demonology' is probably no coincidence, especially considering its connections to Western, Christian ideas of witchcraft, malevolence, and Satanism, and, of course, the demon's position as the diametric opposite of the angel. Malice, spite, and danger are all attributes associated with demons, and over the years, they have combined with the 'mystery' that is the Orient to manifest in a concern that Asian women might use their feminine wiles and 'exotic beauty' to seduce Western, white (read: more civilised) men into submission.

Asian women in Western countries are 'objects of cross-cultural anxiety',[7] notes Professor Ien Ang, the founding director of the Institute for Culture and Society at Western Sydney University, whose work explores issues of migration, ethnicity, diaspora, and representation. Shirley Tucker, a former lecturer at the University of Queensland who completed a PhD on Asian Australian writers, agrees, noting that Asian

---

* As a term, Orientalism refers to the often negative and prejudiced representations of the East by the West, and the ramifications of such portrayals as it relates to power, especially in postcolonial nation-states.

Australian women are often seen as figures 'of the sinful and morally corrupt Asian femme fatale, and the passive and childlike oriental flower'.[8] We are, in essence, a cultural version of Schrödinger's cat – at once docile and dangerous, depending on who we're with or what we're doing.

If we are loud and assertive, then we are the tiger mother or the dragon lady; if we are quiet, then we must be the Oriental flower. There is no in-between for Asian women, no space for us to be normal or mediocre or complex or to just *be*. This is why I've been hesitant to write about this side of my mum. In the past, I would have been less forgiving; I'd be full of accusations and rage with little to no justification. It wouldn't have been fair to either of us. But now I feel like I have the appropriate distance from her and the emotional maturity to be honest without being cruel. I just don't want her to be pigeonholed into a stereotype. She's a whole woman, after all.

Even though my parents taught me all about Chinese superstitions, I didn't know anything about Malaysian folklore or demons until I read Beth Yahp's novel *The Crocodile Fury* (Angus & Robertson, 1992) in my last year of university. I was excited to share my new-found knowledge with my parents, if only because it would mean less time for them to ask me questions I didn't want to answer about my financial situation and whether or not I'd managed to get a boyfriend.

'啊, 對了, 有那個 pontianak,' my dad said, as I butchered the pronunciation. '也有別的, 好像 kuntilanak, 不過那是馬

來人的傳統.' My parents don't believe in ghosts – other than the Holy Spirit, of course – but they still know the legends and the stories of the place they used to call home.

The pontianak presents herself in the shape of a beautiful woman, only revealing herself to be a demon once she gets close to her target. She has long, dark hair, red eyes, long fingernails, and pale skin, which complements her white dress. She smells of plumeria and lures wayward men to their deaths by imitating the sounds of a crying baby, before sucking the life out of them, not unlike the Western concept of the vampire. She eats men's organs – sometimes even their penises, if she is exacting revenge on a specific man – and she can only be defeated by plunging a nail into the back of her head, which transforms her into a beautiful woman and dutiful wife. She is a monster, albeit one with a past: pontianaks are said to be the spirits of women who died while pregnant.

Pontianaks, like other feminine-coded ghosts across Asia, are commonly used to comment on and critique Western imperialism and the patriarchy at large. As Melbourne-based essayist Stephanie Lai notes, they 'give an avenue through which a woman's identity, and a society's boundaries, can be played with, stretched, realised and destroyed. She can maintain her monstrosity, and so can society; but it is a reflection of where she has come from and where she is going.'[9] Singaporean novelist Sharlene Teo's award-winning debut, *Ponti* (Simon & Schuster, 2018), uses the pontianak to do just this. Teo explores capitalism and the commodification of women's bodies through the perspectives of three women in Singapore: Szu; her mother,

Amisa; and Szu's childhood friend, Circe. *Ponti*, the novel's title, is not only short for pontianak, but is also the name of a trilogy of horror movies starring Amisa that were made in the late seventies. Circe, a social media consultant, is put on a project to rejuvenate this trilogy for a modern-day audience, and the project stirs up memories of the Amisa she knew, as well as her relationship with Szu. The novel jumps between the present, the past, and the not-so-distant future, adding to a sense of unease that permeates the narrative.

In an interview with Indonesian short story writer and novelist Intan Paramaditha, Teo notes that 'figures of fear and horror are pariahs and ciphers for insecurity and fear – they reflect what is found, at the time, to be undesirable or repugnant [...] the monster, the neighborhood menace – is the big looming Other'.[10] Horror and the Gothic have always gone hand in hand, possibly because they force us to confront the horrors in our everyday lives that we would rather ignore or suppress. In the past, these horrors may have been vampires or witches, but these days, they're more real than we would like: racism, sexism, elitism, capitalism.

I didn't believe in monsters when I was a kid, with the exception of maybe Satan. Even then, I was still mildly sceptical. The only culturally relevant 'demon' or monster I'd been told about was 年, the monster that used to roam villages to hunt for children every new year before the villagers managed to drive it back by wearing the colour red and banging on drums and setting off firecrackers. My parents told me about 年 and the normal

Chinese superstitions even though they didn't believe in them: don't sweep on New Year's Eve because you'll sweep your good luck out of the house; eat fish on New Year's Eve because 魚 sounds like 餘, the word for wealth; the number eight is lucky and the number four unlucky.

I didn't question any of these beliefs. I knew they weren't 'true' in the complete sense of the word, but I did and do still believe in them, to an extent. I believed my parents, because I was a kid, and why wouldn't I trust them? But when you're young, it's hard to differentiate respect from fear, especially when it comes to adults, let alone authority figures like parents. Maybe with everything else going on in my life – racism, bullying, feeling left out – I had to believe my family and our house was a safe space. Maybe that's how I rationalised the caning, how I still rationalise the caning, sometimes.

It was too hard for me to believe my parents could be monsters, too.

Recently, as my dad was driving me home from dinner, he admitted that he regretted hitting us so much when we were children. We were near an intersection on Mains Road, stopped at a traffic light he'd run a decade or so ago while explaining a complicated maths problem to me. He told me how happy he was that my sister and I had grown into such great adults, how proud he was of us. As he continued to navigate the traffic, he told me he wished he'd given us a more carefree childhood, that if he could do it all again, he'd make sure we had more time to play and go on holidays. I struggled to keep back my tears, knowing a sob might break his train of thought. He'd always been a man of few words, and I wanted to give him the chance to talk for as long as he wanted or needed.

I was touched by his admission, and even more so when my sister told me they'd had a similar conversation. I'd always known my dad to have a kind heart, even if his outward expressions and actions might have suggested otherwise. Still, I know it must have been hard for him to admit any of this out loud to one daughter, let alone two, and I am grateful he shared his thoughts with us.

As much as I would like to hear something similar from my mum, I don't think it will happen any time soon, if at all. She is stubborn; an admission of guilt would imply she'd been wrong, and god forbid she be seen as fallible to her children.

Even though my relationship with my mother is slowly improving, she's yet to master the art of easing into a conversation. In 2020, about ten days before Lunar New Year, she sent me a text. I'd just arrived at work, and I saw her name pop up on my phone. 婆婆 (阿姨的媽媽) 過世了, 葬禮是今天早上, 我們送去了這花, she wrote, with an accompanying photo of the flower arrangement.

婆婆 was the mother of Aunty Lina, a close family friend. We'd go to her place in Oxley every year for Lunar New Year, and sometimes Dad would brave the steep driveway, driving down while knowing he'd have to reverse all the way up when we left. 婆婆 was always there, a constant among the revolving door of Aunty Lina's other family members who would visit for varying lengths of time, smiling and laughing and talking to my parents or us in Cantonese-tinged Mandarin.

I stared at my phone, trying to process the news, and it hit me: I never even knew her name.

My sister and I chatted about it later that afternoon. 'I would have gone to the funeral,' I said. 'I'm a bit annoyed Mum didn't tell me earlier.'

'Yeah, that's the way she operates though – can't say I'm surprised,' my sister replied. 'But like, at least let us write on a card or something.'

We talked about the paper frogs 婆婆 used to make after dinner was done, the way she'd make them jump across the table, much to our amusement. She'd beam at us whenever she gave us our 紅包, and we'd be too embarrassed to peek inside to see how much she'd given us that year.

My sister is the only other person in the world who understands what it is like to be a daughter to my parents, who understands how difficult it can be to talk to Mum. Even then, she has a very different relationship with our mother than I do. She might be annoyed at Mum's or Dad's antics, but I don't think she has an ingrained fear of them or of the house. Mum was gentler to her during her adolescence and young adulthood, especially after I moved out – one of the perks of being the younger sibling. Maybe it was because her personality wasn't as similar to Mum's as mine, or maybe it was simply because my parents didn't want her to leave abruptly, like I did. I don't begrudge her this; I'm glad at least one of us could have something of a normal relationship with Mum.

I see a lot of myself in my sister, but we are also very different. My sister says she thinks I have more of Mum in me than she does. She's probably right, despite the fact that there are also massive differences between us. I wonder how much of Mum – her spirit, her personality, her values – will last. I wonder how much of the person I know as my mother are reflections of the generations of women who have come before her. I wonder if she'll leave us something we can hold on to long after she's gone, something we can pass on to our own daughters if we have them. I think I won't be able to help it; she's so embedded in my DNA, so central to who I am as a person.

Mum and I share a love for reading and writing, and she certainly encouraged me to write when I was younger. I think it's why, despite our long-running animosity, I feel closer to my mother, even though I share a birthday with Dad and I spent more time with him as a child, courtesy of his stay-at-home status. But Mum rarely tells us stories about her childhood. When she does, it's usually for her benefit, to illustrate a point about how lucky we are, how we should be grateful for everything we have.

She tells stories of vying to be top of her class, how the other kids treated her differently because she was a year younger than everyone else. I think she viewed these stories as motivational fodder – *if I was able to do this, you can too!* – but to me, they only served to emphasise how different our environments were. I had no desire to do or be better than anyone else – the concept of competitiveness was foreign to me. She once lamented not teaching me to have a competitive streak, never mind the consequences of such behaviour or even if competitiveness was a teachable trait.

Mum also brought out her anecdotes to tell us why she made specific decisions – '因為我小的時候, 公公從來不准我們孩子出去做這個還是那個的, 所以媽媽對你們比較輕鬆一點.' She didn't want us to go through the same restrictions that were placed on her by her father, but didn't realise or seem to take into account that growing up in suburban Brisbane in the noughties was different to growing up in rural Malaysia in the sixties and seventies.

I used to tell her stories, too. When I was younger, I'd tell her what happened at school, about my friends and the bullies, what I'd learnt that day. But I stopped when she started using my anecdotes against me, to tell me my behaviour and my actions were why I didn't have any friends, and why I was bullied so much. I also didn't tell her the stories I really wanted to – stories about playing *Mario Kart* during chemistry, or skipping physics to hang out with the music kids – because I knew she would disapprove, and with that disapproval would come some form of punishment.

These days, we are emotionally estranged, even though I only live a thirty-minute drive away. It's taken me a long time to begin to trust her again, and I'm not sure if she knows how brittle this trust really is. I make sure to tell her enough about my life that she's satisfied, but not too much lest she begin asking more probing questions. It's a careful balance.

After I started *Pencilled In*, my solo venture into the world of literary magazine publishing, Mum told me she used to write for a national newspaper in Malaysia. 'It only paid about ten ringgit, you know,' she said. 'You couldn't make a living in the arts in Malaysia at that time – there was no government funding. So I went to university.' She implied that she went to university to study something that would lead to a career, not for something as frivolous as the arts. I wanted to pry more, but I knew it would be futile. Mum only shares on her terms.

Mum softens a little when she tells stories these days, even if it is something banal, like a story of a particular patient she's seen. She's more animated, too, more *human*. The edges of her face seem smoother, and her smile seems gentler. Maybe it's because I get to see some of myself in my mum when she's in storytelling mode.

I want to know more about *that* version of my mum.

Like many daughters, I worry I will become my mother some day. This transformation would be incremental, not unlike something out of a horror movie or a ghost story – my mother's ghost, come to haunt me while she is still alive. I can already see parts of us moulding together: the way we both repeat a story if we think it's of particular note, the way we can come to the same solution for a problem, the way we both think long-sleeved tops with cold shoulders are silly and should be banned from all shops.

I know that if I have children, I'd want them to go to Chinese school and to abacus classes, just as she did with us. I know I will never hit my children, but I might find a different way to scare them into submission. Who knows what tools I will be able to access in the future for these purposes? I worry I will have good intentions, but fumble at their execution. I don't want my children to fear me like I do my own mother.

But I also know I would be lost without my mum. I wouldn't know how to name my children properly in Chinese, because these are secrets I have not been privy to; I don't know which traditions I should be upholding. I wouldn't know the right words or even the right combination of words to use.

I know that in some ways I have no right to criticise my mum. After all, I have no idea what it's like to be a mother, let alone a mother in a different country with a different language and culture while single-handedly running a business. Maybe she had to be this way to get shit done. But there will always be a part of me that wonders why my voice matters less than hers simply by virtue of being her daughter. We will never be equals; our conversations will never really be discussions between two adults.

This might seem unfair, but maybe it's the way things have to be, at least for now. Maybe I'll feel differently as I age, as I morph into a hybrid of my mother and my own self. I can only hope this hybrid is neither demon nor pontianak.

5

Language

It is fifteen minutes to midnight, and I have just arrived in Jaipur. I am bleary-eyed, tired, and hungry – I have been on planes and in airports for the past twenty or so hours. My taxi driver speaks a little English and kindly tries to tell me which landmarks I should visit, even though I know I won't remember the conversation, let alone the names of the places, in the morning. When I get to the hostel, it is half-past midnight. I've always imagined India as a place crammed with people and noise and energy, but in the dark it is almost peaceful, despite the hum that simmers through the city and the glare of the lights along the streets.

The next day, I decide to venture out by myself, and it is overwhelming. I am reminded, all too painfully, that I am a young woman in India, travelling abroad on my own for the first time, surrounded by too many people, with men staring at me wherever I go. The language is different – grating, yet reminiscent of the melody and rhythm of Mandarin – and the air around me is different, too – dusty, sandy, gold, and, at times, slightly pink (though this might just be an illusion courtesy of the Hawa Mahal). I am not scared, but I am anxious. I don't know when I should feel safe. I don't fully understand the social contracts at play – when or if it's okay to ignore someone, how much space I should leave between me and the person in front of me when I'm in a queue, if I'm within my rights to yell at someone who's claimed the tuk-tuk I've hailed – and it's not like I can just go up to someone in the street and ask. I second-guess my instincts.

I start talking to myself – inside my head – in an effort to calm my thumping heart. Surprisingly, most of this internal dialogue is conducted in Mandarin. 你還可以, 嗎? 還可以啦. 走啊, 走. 走快一點, 慢一點. 不要管他的, 喔? I sound like a chiding auntie. I tell myself I am going to be okay, that everything is going be all right. I start narrating my actions and describing my surroundings. 小心, 他在看你喔. 那裡的衣服很漂亮, 因該進去看看? 看一下吧. 好, 好, 不要買就走啦. 不管他的, 喔? It is my way of staying grounded – of not losing myself, physically and figuratively.

While I'm in India, I even think in Mandarin for brief periods of time. At first, it is disconcerting, but it becomes something of a balm. In a way, it is nice to know I haven't lost my language, that nuggets of it still remain. There are other Chinese tourists at the hostel, and I talk to them in an attempt to make them feel more comfortable. But as the days roll on, I find that it is me who is becoming more comfortable.

Some people go to India to try to 'find themselves', to have a life-changing, spiritual experience. I went to India for a literary festival, and re-found something I already had: my love for Mandarin, my first language.

Mandarin is the language my parents actively taught me when I was little – it was the only language I was allowed to speak at home, and I also attended Chinese school from a young age. There's a little more leeway for English now that I'm older, but I'm still expected to speak to my parents mostly in Mandarin. When I was a toddler, Mum had made a box of flashcards, full of nouns and idioms and pronunciations. This box had formerly carried mango and vanilla ice creams from the Home Ice Cream van, but it was now full to the brim with cards, the strong, black strokes of my mother's handwriting imprinting onto my brain. I don't know where that box is now. Maybe it's somewhere in the depths of my parents' too-large house; maybe my dad has hoarded it somewhere like he hoards golf clubs he won't use and tables he's picked up during kerbside collection. Maybe it's just gone.

My three-year-old self knew more Mandarin than my current self. Apparently, I did a test when I was three (I have no memory of this, but I've seen the results), which showed my Mandarin language skills were off the charts for my age, but my English wasn't so great. Nowadays, if I'm speaking in

Mandarin, I have to think sentences through before I open my mouth. I take longer to process Mandarin during a conversation than I would like, and I usually have to concentrate more than I would if I was having the same conversation in English. When I read a news article or a short section of a book that's written in Chinese, I feel slow. There are some words I can't pronounce, others that I can guess at because of the way they're constructed – sometimes characters that are written similarly have similar meanings, or one character I don't recognise might have within it another character I'm familiar with, and I can then try to muddle out its meaning. Most of the time I can figure out the gist of a sentence through context, but not knowing how to pronounce a word or a phrase is still infuriating, especially for someone who reads by speaking out the words in their head.

My parents have varying degrees of fluency in English, Mandarin Chinese, Fuchow (a dialect of Chinese), and Bahasa Melayu. They can also understand Cantonese, Hokkien, and Bahasa Indonesia. Conversations at home would be held in a mixture of Mandarin and Fuchow, with the odd English word or phrase thrown in. This means I'm very comfortable with switching languages mid-sentence, but it also means my languages are a little mixed up.

Chinese is a non-phonetic language, as are all its dialects, which complicates matters even further. There are many people who can understand and speak Mandarin, or a dialect of Chinese, but have no idea how to read or write characters. Others were only taught simplified characters, which renders anything written in traditional Chinese almost foreign. My own reading and writing skills in Chinese are far poorer than my speaking and listening skills. I probably couldn't deliver a formal speech in Mandarin, but I can hold my own in a free-flowing conversation. I could write a letter to a friend or a diary entry, but probably not a poem or an essay. Even though I have these skills, there are still some aspects of the language that seem beyond my grasp – there are so many idioms I haven't encountered, let alone understood to the point where I can slip them into casual conversation, so much history and meaning couched in seemingly ordinary characters and phrases.

For example, I don't know the phrase for garlic in Mandarin, but I know it in Fuchow. I thought the Fuchow word for bread was 'lo-di' until well into my teenage years, when my parents told me that was actually Bahasa Melayu (from 'roti'). I don't know the word for cheese in Mandarin. My sister jokes that one of the only phrases she knows how to say in Fuchow is 'Have you practised the piano yet?' simply by virtue of the number of times this was asked of her. Because I have these gaps in my knowledge of Mandarin, I tend to code-switch. I'm using the linguistic, as opposed to the cultural, definition of code-switching here, one that linguist Shana Poplack defines as 'the mixing, by bilinguals (or multilinguals), of two or more languages in discourse, often with no change of interlocutor or topic'.[1] I do this quite often, sometimes without even really thinking about it. If I don't know how to say something in Mandarin, I will switch to English, then back again. Sometimes I try to translate something directly from English to Mandarin even though I know I shouldn't, and then before I know it the grammar is all wrong and tangled and I don't know how to fix it, so I get stuck and flustered and have to finish the sentence in English.

My Mandarin has worsened since I moved away from my parents – a necessary move for my mental wellbeing. I didn't get along with my parents particularly well before I left, and I tried to avoid them as much as possible, but the consistent hum of Mandarin still hung in the background, reinforcing those flashcard lessons and two decades of exposure to the language. Mandarin is my first language, even though it doesn't feel like it anymore, even though I speak English fluently, 'like an Australian' – whatever that's supposed to mean.

The last time I filled out my census form, I stumbled over the question, *Does the person use a language other than English at home?* I've come across many versions of this question before, so I knew it was coming, but I didn't know how to answer it properly. This sort of question makes sense as part of the census, but when it's in staff or student surveys it makes me feel strange. The way it's couched in strangely formulaic language signals an attempt at politeness, a tiptoeing around the real question: *Are you white?*

When I lived at home, I'd tick the 'yes' box, but now I live alone, and I have done so for the better part of the last decade. When I'm on my own, I mostly speak to myself in English, I mostly read in English, I mostly watch English television shows and movies. I remember looking over at one of my cats, who was curled up on the couch next to me, and thinking, *I mostly talk to my cats in English, too.* These days, Mandarin is still a big part of my life and my identity, but, comparatively, I know and use so little of it.

And what little I do know is being slowly eaten away.

I know I am lucky. I know many children of immigrants can't communicate in their parents' languages, and I know this results in a loss of identity they can't ever really get back. I know there's a certain privilege in my parents having the money to send me to Chinese school in the first place, even if I wasn't a big fan of having my Saturday mornings ripped away from me for years on end.

In Weike Wang's novel *Chemistry*, the protagonist says she feels more comfortable in English, even though Eric, her boyfriend, says he can tell she's not a native English speaker. 'You say *close* for everything,' he says. 'Close the lights, the TV, the oven. You say *close* when you really mean *turn off.*' In response, she thinks, 'Because in Chinese, there is only one word for it. *Guan.*'[2]

Reading this prompted a pang of recognition. I used to tell M to 'close the lights' so often that it became a running joke, and I'd probably been telling other people to close the lights for years before he pointed it out to me.

I know I am lucky to have the ability to make this mistake in the first place, but is it greedy of me to want more? Is it ungrateful of me to be annoyed or upset at the fact that I'm not 'truly fluent'? I wonder what a grown-up version of my three-year-old self would be like. Language influences the way we think, the way we approach the world. Would I be a different person if I knew more Mandarin, if I knew how to write more characters, if I engaged with the language on a deeper level? Would that person be a better, wiser, more knowledgeable version of who I am now?

The loss of a native language is usually referred to as 'language attrition'. It doesn't necessarily refer to a complete loss of language – most of the time, it just means more pauses and mistakes when speaking the language at hand. Monika Schmid, a professor of linguistics at the University of York, and Barbara Köpke, a professor of neurolinguistics at the University of Toulouse in France, define language attrition as a phenomenon that occurs when someone's first language 'becomes less accessible or is modified to some extent as a result of the acquisition of a new language'.[3] Schmid also says many characteristics of 'what is called language attrition are quite similar to changes in language use often found in very early stages of dementia' – although she does also point out that they are neurologically different, and that 're-immersion in the native language will probably make them disappear within a few weeks'.[4]

The knowledge that my Mandarin could come back to me with re-immersion is comforting, but it is still confronting to be thrown into an environment where you feel 'lesser than' if you can't communicate properly in your first language. And that's even before you consider the fact that you can't really be yourself – you can't pepper your conversations with your usual sarcasm or cheek – simply because you aren't able to manipulate that language the way you can in English. In the case of Mandarin and other Chinese dialects, the language exists in a culture where maintaining and saving face is an almost ingrained trait – not being able to speak it at all is preferable to speaking it, and speaking it badly. Knowing you will never be truly proficient in a language may be enough to discourage people from continuing to learn the language or may prevent them from attempting it in the first place. Language attrition, then, seems like the natural way of things for people like me – children of parents who migrated to Western societies.

Studies in language attrition have looked at adults, migrants, children, international adoptees, refugees, and the elderly. It is most prevalent among people who are bilingual, especially people who were raised in households like mine – one language spoken at home, but surrounded by English speakers in an English-speaking society, with television programs and books and movies in English. To be honest, I don't even know if I really am bilingual anymore, in the truest sense of the term.

The pressure to assimilate or integrate in Western countries like Australia can be so strong that people forgo their first languages completely, and do not pass them on to their children. In *Second Languages and Australian Schooling*, a review published in 2009 for the Australian Council for Educational Research, Joseph Lo Bianco, with assistance from Yvette

Slaughter, identifies four stages of bilingualism in immigrant Australian communities: '(i) first language dominance (or monolingualism) in the language other than English; (ii) bilingualism in the community language plus English; (iii) English language dominance with diminished first language competence and use; (iv) English monolingualism.'[5] In a stunning twist of irony, Lo Bianco has the audacity to accuse these people, who may have rejected their first languages as a matter of survival, of ripping off the government, writing, 'In a perfect model of wastefulness some children, having lost knowledge of the home language, available to the society at no cost to the public purse, are then offered the same language in schools as beginner learners of a taught foreign language.'[6] This seeming lack of empathy for the myriad reasons why these children might not know their 'home language' reflects a lack of understanding when it comes to migrant and diasporic experiences, and is exacerbated by the bizarre capitalist phenomenon of attaching a monetary value to language.

My parents have both been in Australia for over twenty years, and my mum is now an Australian citizen. They are both multilingual, and were fairly insistent that their children would be proficient in Mandarin. Because our house was a strictly non–English speaking space, my sister and I would make our own little inside jokes that basically involved us combining English words with their Mandarin counterparts and chanting them so we wouldn't get in trouble for speaking English at home. '叔叔阿姨看到你就以為你們會講華語，不會講就好丟臉喔!' my parents reminded us often, especially when they admonished us for our increasing use of English. Now I understand it was as much about saving their own face among their peers as it was about saving ours.

Even though they insisted on us learning Mandarin, my parents still had some sort of awareness, whether it was conscious or otherwise, of the racist nature of white Australians, despite the country's claims of tolerance and multiculturalism. 'Don't speak Mandarin in front of people who can't understand it,' Dad would say, when I spoke to him in Mandarin while we were in close proximity to white people. 'It's rude and disrespectful.' At the time, I liked the idea of being able to speak in a language that was just for us, and I didn't understand why he didn't feel the same. But now I see this as another case of migrants silencing themselves and making themselves smaller for the benefit of those who are, for whatever reason, afraid or suspicious of people who don't look and sound like them.

Now I live on my own, I try to maintain my hold on Mandarin by doing little things like texting my parents in Chinese, setting my phone language as Chinese, and going to Chinese-run restaurants and eavesdropping on other people's conversations. I also want to go to China for a year to teach English to improve my Mandarin. Ironically, I've heard countless times that it's exponentially harder for a Chinese-presenting person to snag one of these gigs than it is a white person. These small efforts mean I can hold conversations on any number of topics, but I can always feel myself slipping backwards – inserting an

English word here or there, or needing to use some form of translation service for phrases that seem blindingly obvious once I have the translation.

I also try reading Chinese books. I like reading in English, so it made sense that I would like reading in Chinese, too. A few years ago, I checked out a book from the local library in an attempt to improve (or at the very least, maintain) my reading skills. It wasn't a picture book, but wasn't a dense novel either. It looked like a young adult novel, or maybe the Chinese version of a trashy paperback. I liked the cover, so I checked it out and curled up on the couch with it. I took notes as I read; in one column, I wrote out words and phrases that I couldn't pronounce, but had figured out the meanings for from context. In another column were words and phrases I couldn't pronounce, and for which I also had not managed to figure out the meanings. When I finished the book, I texted my mother, asking her for pronunciations and to confirm meanings. She obliged, but also texted back, 你可能要讀比較簡單的書, 吧? 家裡有很多, 應該回來拿一些. I was offended by the insinuation that I'd been reading something that was too advanced for me, especially because I simply wanted confirmation from a human as opposed to a digital dictionary. I was also suspicious of her offer for me to come home – I couldn't help but think, *It's a trap!* I was torn between wanting to learn more and risking a lecture (or worse) from my mum. In the end, I tried to double-down on the reading, but I didn't text her again to ask for clarification.

There's so much I wish I could talk to my mother about, whether it be in Mandarin or English.

I wish I could talk to my mother about sex. I wish I could talk to her about my relationships, about how confused and annoyed and excited I feel when I think I might like someone. In movies and television shows, mothers are confidantes for their daughters, despite the fraught nature of adolescence. They have their issues, but they also have heart-to-hearts that end in hugs and tears – or, at the very least, a sense of mutual understanding. I want that closeness, that intimacy with my mother. I know that at a very base level she loves me with all her heart and she wants the best for me, but I've never heard her say that out loud. I also know that this is the way things are – this is the way things have to be, because of Chinese culture and her upbringing – but it doesn't stop me from wishing nonetheless.

Mum has only ever given me relationship advice once. At the end of year twelve, she told me to find a boyfriend at university (the implication being we'd then stay together forever and get married), because it would be easier to find someone then as opposed to when I was working. She also told me boys don't like it when girls are smarter than them. I laughed it off at the time, but as I got older, I realised how right she was on both counts. Unsurprisingly, my teenage self did not heed her advice. She rarely commented on my relationship with M (she only saw him twice during the nearly three years we were together), and didn't really say anything about finding someone to settle down with after we broke up – even though I know she still sees my future as one where I have a nuclear family and a big, comfortable house.

I wish I could talk to my mother about sex, but I understand why it will probably never happen – it would require a degree of vulnerability from both of us that I don't think either of us is currently willing to relinquish. I wish I could talk to my mother about sex, but I can't, because I literally do not know the words or phrases in Mandarin. I could talk to her about it in English, but somehow that seems wrong – especially after a childhood full of 'no English at home'. I still feel weird talking to her in English now, even in casual conversation. Maybe it's because I want to save face, or maybe it's because of some twisted sense of filial piety. Talking to her about sex in English feels even more wrong than talking about it in the first place.

I wish I could have talked to my mother about sex when I was younger, because I had so many questions. I *have* so many questions. There are questions that can't be answered by a quick Google search, or even by asking some of my friends. Questions about what it is like to date as an Asian woman, how to keep your wits about you in an environment that seems so very foreign, what to do when you're in a relationship and you come up against certain obstacles. I wish I could talk to my mother about how difficult it was to get M to understand our culture. I wish I could have asked for suggestions on how to bridge that gap – but how could I, when I didn't even know how to bridge the gap between us?

I wish I could talk to my mother about all of this, but I can't, because I'm not supposed to have sex before I get married. It contravenes the laws of Christianity, and crosses a line when it comes to traditional Chinese culture. I'm also too scared of history repeating itself, of my parents taking my experiences and vulnerabilities, storing them and using them against me later. I shouldn't talk to them about sex, or anything that's even remotely related to sex, because I've only just begun to be comfortable around them again, after years of wondering what I could say to them without triggering a lecture or a sly barb at the way I live my life.

In any case, I don't even know how I would start that conversation.

'媽媽, 我要跟你討論一下 … sex?'

I don't even know how to say 'sex' in Mandarin.

Language attrition refers to the loss of a native language, but is there a term that describes the phenomenon of not being able to talk about a specific topic, simply because you never learnt the words to begin with?

When I was around six or seven, Mum taught me Mandarin at home for a couple of years. I'd been going to the church's Chinese school, but she was concerned that I'd get picked on in class because everyone else there was at least a few years older than me. She was a hard taskmaster. I had to write essays every week, on grid paper she made herself in a Microsoft Word document on our old PC that still ran Windows 98. It was a poor imitation of the exercise books I used at Chinese school, which were used from right to left, top to bottom, with squares that didn't make me squish my characters so they would fit, and rectangles beside them for 注音 if I needed it.

I hated having Mum as my Mandarin teacher. I didn't really see the point in it. I understood why it was important, but I disliked how hard it was and how much easier I found English and when was I ever going to use Mandarin outside of home and church, anyway? But Mum was insistent. As a child, she won awards for her writing in both Chinese and English, excelling in the writing of essays and fiction, and she never tired of telling us that the money she won from those essay competitions paid for her schoolbooks and stationery, as well as the Enid Blyton paperbacks we read obsessively as children. She saw potential in me, but she didn't tell me this out loud. She just said, '很重要,' firmly, and calmly, and I was crushed by the weight of generations of inbuilt filial piety.

I don't know where those essays are now – there must be enough to make a book, at least – my juvenilia, Chinese style. I'd like to think they were thrown away, that all the characters I spent so long crafting and trapping in those little squares were, perhaps like Mum's flashcards in that ice-cream box, set free. But knowing my parents – knowing my father – they're probably safely stored somewhere in the depths of their bookshelves, a relic of their elder daughter's childhood and conscientiousness. Maybe they'll pull them out when I'm struggling to teach my own children Mandarin, proof that I was once good at it, but not so much anymore.

Mum still corrects me when she gets the chance. I don't think she can help herself. For example, when I let her know about the status of some pain I'd been having in my chest, I texted, 我今天去了醫生, 這個星期去做 *X-ray.* She replied: 是照 *X-ray,* 不是做 *X-ray.* Part of me was grateful because I knew she was right, but another part of me was annoyed. She was the one who nagged me into going to see the doctor in the first place, but then picked on my phrasing even though she obviously knew what I meant. I knew she was just trying to be helpful, but I still felt a pang of guilt, for a second. Maybe it's because I felt like I had let her down – I couldn't even get the verb for an X-ray right.

Before the advent of easily accessible translation apps, I had to use the Chinese dictionary to find pronunciations and associated phrases. It's a strange, unwieldy creature; the dictionary is sorted by radical – the graphical 'base' or 'root' of each character, which often also provides a hint as to the character's meaning – and the radicals are sorted by number of strokes. Each radical has a section that is carefully numbered. Once you get to the appropriate section – and this is if you're also sure you've pinpointed the correct radical – you can start looking for your desired character. There is a fair bit of counting involved for the use of a Chinese dictionary. From this point I would find the character I wanted by counting the number of strokes needed to write that character, excluding the strokes needed for the radical. Once you find your word, it's like a normal English dictionary – there is a pronunciation guide, albeit in 注音, followed by that word's associated definitions.

It then lists common phrases and idioms beginning with that word. Sometimes there are only a few, but in other cases there are almost too many; for example, in one of my Chinese dictionaries, there are seven and a half pages devoted to the character 一.

This system works perfectly if you have all of the correct information at your disposal – the correct radical (keeping in mind that the form in which a radical presents itself in a particular character may not be the same form you need it in to look it up in the dictionary), the correct number of leftover strokes, and an adequate amount of knowledge to then read and understand the definition or definitions provided. If you're not sure of the meaning of a word in the definition, you have to go on that journey all over again. It seems to be an insular system, and potentially a lot of work for not very much gain.

I was probably eleven or twelve when my parents decided to send me back to Chinese school, and it was there that I learnt how to use a Chinese dictionary. Mine looked like a miniature version of the yellow pages, except full of Chinese characters, and like my textbooks they were read from right to left, top to bottom. When I first got it, the cover was glossy, the spine uncracked. It was full of possibilities, full of new words and characters to learn. Now, it is falling apart. If I don't hold it together when I use it, its pages will collapse, wrench themselves out of the spine and into my hands in two big chunks. My name is written in white-out on the front cover, alongside a love heart that has been coloured in with orange highlighter. When unopened, there are black imprints of Hamtaro, a hamster who is the protagonist of a Japanese manga of the same name, stamped on the pages, probably another symptom of boredom during Chinese classes. My sister's name is written in large, bold characters on the inside cover, and my name is written again underneath hers, but incorrectly, with a 容 instead of a 蓉, in glittery gold pen that was either smudged while my name was being written, or has faded with time.

Even so, I loved that dictionary. I might not have read it in the same way I read my English dictionary, but it opened up a world of possibilities. There were phrases, pronunciations, and idioms I'd never seen or heard before. When I first received this dictionary, I had already resigned myself to the fact I'd never be as fluent as my parents in Mandarin, or understand the nuances of the language like they did, but I knew this dictionary was a tool that could help me on my way.

I read Xiaolu Guo's *A Concise Chinese-English Dictionary for Lovers* (Vintage Arrow, 2008) when I was twenty-three, the same age as the novel's protagonist, Zhuang. In a sense, Zhuang and I had opposing problems. She is trying to learn English, a hybrid, bumbling language with a semblance of grammar, a language that breaks its grammatical rules as often as it follows them. I delighted in reading a novel with a Chinese protagonist who is unapologetic in her explorations of sex, a novel where Chinese characters are at home with English words and sentences.

Zhuang, like me, is trying to figure out what it means to be a sexual being – a sexual woman – in a Western society. Even though she is in London (and a fictional character), and I am in Brisbane, there are similarities in the issues we face by virtue of being Chinese-presenting women in a predominantly white society. Unlike Zhuang, I can communicate in the language of this Western society. I am able to understand the nuances of this thing we call the English language, and, though I am frustrated by my Mandarin abilities, I don't feel too out of place. I am different, but I blend in. I can learn about sex by discreetly reading about it in books and magazines. Zhuang doesn't have that luxury.

Instead, she goes to a sex shop and watches a peep show. She writes of her experience, 'While I am standing there watching, I desire become prostitute. I want be able expose my body, to relieve my body, to take my body away from dictionary and grammar and sentences, to let my body break all disciplines.'[7] The comparatively rigid confines of English, the language she is trying to learn, stifles her ability to communicate, and she desperately wants to find another way to express herself, to connect with someone else. Sex, and eventually love, is one way in which she finds that connection, but even that is not enough to overcome the powerlessness she feels at not being fully able to communicate with her lover.

In a chapter titled 'nonsense', she writes, '我真想說回我天生的語言, 可是, 我天生的語言它是真正的天生的嗎? [...] 我們為甚麼要學語言? 我們為甚麼要強迫自己與他人交流? 如果交流的過程是如此痛苦?'[8] This one-page chapter is written entirely in Chinese, with an editor's translation on the following page. I read the Chinese characters slowly, much slower than I would have if they had been English words. As I read, my brain churning over the words – not translating them into English, but just trying to understand their full meaning – I felt a kinship with Zhuang. She questions the nature of language and if it is innate or god-given, and why we put ourselves through the difficulties of learning languages. She wonders if her first language, the language she was born with, is really her first language, the one she is supposed to speak.

I wonder if Zhuang knows the characters for sex, sexual intercourse, orgasm, and clitoris in Mandarin. I wonder if she had talked to her parents about it. I wonder if she even wants to be able to talk to her parents about it. I marvel at how much we are both alike and, at the same time, very much not alike at all. I wonder what would have happened if Zhuang had come to Australia instead of the UK. I wonder what would have happened if I had been born in Malaysia instead of Australia. Would I have a more expansive sexual vocabulary? Or would I just simply be unable to talk about it in any language? Would it just be a gap in knowledge I didn't even know I had?

I can rattle off at least a dozen euphemisms for sex in English, but I wouldn't have a clue where to start if you asked me to do the same in Mandarin. I don't even know how to swear in my first language, much to the chagrin of the other kids at school, who prided themselves on knowing how to swear in at least ten different languages.

When I was about fourteen, one of the other kids at church accused me, teasingly, of 談戀愛 with one of the other boys. We were playing basketball at the time, and I had just wrestled the ball away from this same boy, one of my oldest friends at church. There was a lot of giggling, denial, and more giggling. I didn't know what this phrase meant, but I was mortified anyway, because of all of the laughing. And because of all of the laughing and the fact that the phrase included the word 愛, I assumed I had been accused of having sex. I didn't want to ask my parents, just in case I was right.

My trusty translation app tells me that the word for sex in Chinese is 性. It makes sense, if I dissect it. The radical for heart, 忄, combined with the character for body, 生. As with all Mandarin words, the pronunciation of 性 is similar to many others. I have probably said it many times without even knowing it. But simply knowing the word isn't enough. I don't really know how to use it in a sentence or in a conversation. I don't know how it can be used. I don't know if there are any 成語 that talk about relationships or sex more elegantly – there probably are, what with their ability to wrap worlds of information into four tiny characters. 'Penis' turns up a bunch of translations, many of them labelled 'vulgar' or 'colloquial'. There is 鳥, 雞巴, 陰莖. A search for 'vagina' gives me 陰道, 石女, 縮陰 – the last of which means 'to make the vagina tighter'. At first, I am taken aback, but it seems par for the course for a language that in some ways is horribly misogynistic; for example, the character for mother, 媽, is a combination of female (女) and horse (馬), and the character for good, 好, a combination of female (女) and son (子).

I use Google Translate for posterity – translation can be finicky, so I want to confirm my results. Google gives me 性, as well as 性交, for sexual intercourse. This seems correct, as 交 means 'to interchange', 'to share'. I recognise how the characters and phrases are put together, but it still doesn't make total sense to me. It occurs to me that Google's translation for 'sex' may be referring to anatomical sex as opposed to 'the act of doing sex', which only confuses me more. Even so, the more I think about Chinese and the way it is constructed, the more I appreciate the language. To share sex – anatomically, or otherwise – seems almost poetic, and it is this inherent beauty in the Chinese language that keeps me coming back to it.

When I came home from India, I was keener than ever to get my Mandarin up to scratch. I was hyperaware of my inadequacy, but I also knew there were remnants of fluency in the deeper recesses of my brain, flickers of remembrance that needed a little push to fully develop. I looked for Chinese schools that taught traditional characters, and tried to find places that would cater to people of my skill level and age. There weren't (and still aren't) many in Brisbane, though I found a few in Sydney and Melbourne. A friend suggested I go to meet-ups with Chinese international students to practise, but that wouldn't cover the reading and writing side of things. Though I felt like I'd be lying to myself if I only ever knew a sanitised version of what is essentially my first language, I wanted to *learn*, and not just so I could say rude words or have inappropriate conversations. I wanted to learn more 成語, more about the intricacies of this language that has retained many of its roots from ancient times.

I ended up rummaging around my parents' house for my old Chinese school books. I had grand plans to use them to ease myself back into learning more Chinese. When I found them, I was both excited and embarrassed – it turned out I'd only ever reached a grade five standard of reading and writing. Twelve-year-olds would show me up. These slim volumes were the textbooks we'd take to each class, and they bear remnants of my bored teenage self – on one, I have traced the title, 國語, in white-out, and coloured the white space in the characters with pink and orange highlighter. I have also scribbled and doodled with highlighter and sparkly gel pen on the inside and, in more than one chapter, I have traced over the outlines of all the images in white-out. This doesn't mean I wasn't a diligent student – I have also highlighted phrases and 成語 and written out their English translations alongside them. 炎熱 (very x100 hot)/嬌綠 (very, very green)/讚不絕口 (very good, so good that it cannot be described)/蜿蜒 (like wiggling) – the list goes on.

When I rifle through one particular textbook, I see that it contains poetry, letters, short plays, stories, and essays. It is far more comprehensive than any English reading I did at school when I was in grade five. Each piece follows a similar format, education-wise. A series of words sit atop the piece itself – they are the words I would learn that week, the words

I would be tested on the following week. As I flick through the textbook, I realise that I don't recognise many of those words, and I probably wouldn't be able to pronounce them if they didn't have 注音 written next to them.

I never studied past fifth grade at Chinese school because high school and other commitments overwhelmed my Saturdays, and my parents decided it would be a better use of my time and their money to employ a Chinese tutor to come to our house every week for an hour for Chinese lessons. Even so, I wonder if textbooks in the grades above covered sex or relationships in any way, or if they continued to avoid such topics, as is customary in Chinese culture.

In some ways, all my wondering about this seems facetious. People don't learn how to swear or talk about so-called inappropriate subjects like sex from textbooks. They learn from their environment, from absorbing snippets of sentences from passers-by, or eavesdropping on conversations at the table next to them in a restaurant. Even in English schools, discussions around sex are not embedded in the curriculum – aside from the occasional mandatory sex-education class, which seems to be more of a hotbed for snickering at the words 'penis' and 'vagina' and any other variant thereof than for any actual education to take place.

Xiaolu Guo's Zhuang asks why we bother to learn languages – why we bother to learn new languages. Is it just so we can communicate with one another? Or is it simply because learning another language might provide ways in which we can attempt to empathise with those who seem to be different from us? But maybe that's just wishful thinking. Maybe it has nothing to do with empathy at all.

When I was told I had to study a language in high school, I chose Chinese. My teacher was tough – much tougher than the teachers at Chinese school. He said he was deliberately setting difficult tasks for us so we'd find the final exam easy, which seemed like ample justification for all the red marks I got whenever my homework essays were handed back. I was halfway through some Chinese homework in year eleven when Mum showed me a dictionary – 'a daily use English-Chinese dictionary'. It was bound in bright blue, and the spine creaked when I opened it. The pages were a wooden brown colour, and the alphabet was splayed out across its pages in an S-shape, the size of each letter corresponding to the number of pages devoted to that particular subset of words. Mum's name was written below these meandering letters in exact calligraphy, a far cry from my almost-globular white-out graffiti of my own name on the front cover of my dictionary. It was typeset in what looked like an old version of Courier New in a very small font, and the Chinese characters were squished in even smaller – so much so that I felt like I would probably need a magnifying glass to read it properly. Mum told me her father gave her this dictionary. She didn't need it anymore, but she thought it would be useful for me to have.

I used it a few times, before Google Translate and all manner of translation apps came along and both of my Chinese dictionaries were relegated to the bookshelf, objects for display purposes only. But when I moved out, I insisted on taking them with me. Maybe I thought they would enable me to keep hold of my roots, or they would come in handy sometime when I had lost my phone and my wi-fi was down. Or maybe I just wanted them as a reminder of home.

At the end of 2020, the Australian government implemented stricter English language tests as part of the application for Australian citizenship. In a keynote address at the Menzies Research Centre in 2018, Alan Tudge, the Minister for Citizenship, stated that even though 'Australia is the most successful multicultural country in the world [...] Australian multiculturalism is not God-given and cannot be taken for granted'.[9] Such a claim to multiculturalism is laughable, especially considering the ongoing atrocities committed against Aboriginal and Torres Strait Islander people, offshore detention policies, and the White Australia policy, which was abolished only a short time ago. Scott Morrison, the Prime Minister at the time, took pride in the fact that the new test would require potential citizens to have stronger English language skills. He justified this by claiming 'people's employment outcomes [...] rapidly increase if they have got a good strong command of English [...] This puts an even greater emphasis on English language. It is in their interest, in Australia's interests, it is our national language.'[10]

Putting aside the fact Australia doesn't have an official

language, many white Australians agree with Morrison's sentiment. That is, if people are going to live in Australia, they'd better learn how to speak English, and to speak it well – which begs the question, does knowing more English really make me more Australian? If so, I'd be willing to bet that I'm more Australian than a lot of the white Australians who profess to be 'true-blue Aussies'. Does knowing more Chinese, or Mandarin, or any other Chinese dialect make me more Chinese? I don't think so – at least, not at this moment in time. Does not knowing typical Australian slang make me less Australian? And if so, is it the same as saying that not knowing how to talk about sex in Mandarin makes me less Chinese than someone else who does? These questions are interesting hypotheticals, but that's where they should remain. A person's identity should not solely be constrained by their ability to speak a particular language, or even their understanding of that language, and it should never be regulated or legislated. Identities, after all, are fluid, and should remain so.

Beth Yahp, a Malaysian Chinese Australian writer of fiction, essays, and memoir, writes, 'the personal curse of the Chinese is to be surrounded by a myriad unnamed things'.[11] The mix of dialects our family speaks and the hybridity of the language I grew up with means there are so many things that are named and yet also unnamed. I know barely any of my family medical history – it only ever seems to come up when I say I've been to the doctor for something, and one or both of my parents will pipe up with another morsel of important medical information that would have been useful before my appointment.

I only know snippets of my parents' childhoods, and they only know snippets of my adulthood. There are things that are unnamed simply because it is too hard to put the feeling or the action or the idea into words, and forcing it into a phrase or even a saying would not do it any justice. And there are things that will always remain unnamed because to name them is to make them real.

I wonder if my mother wishes she could talk to me about sex. I wonder what she would want to say, if she could. I wonder if it would be more than a lecture, more than a chance to tell me to be wary of boys and their wily ways, and not to be pressured into anything I wasn't comfortable with. I wonder if the conversation would extend much further than having children and starting a family. This isn't something I'd be averse to, but I would be lying if I said I was okay with that being the sole focus of discussion if we were to talk in any depth about sex or any of my relationships. For now, I'm content with chuckling awkwardly whenever she asks me if and when I'm going to get married.

Maybe, understandably, Mum doesn't want to be able to talk to me about sex. We already keep so many things from one another, secrets slipped in behind pockets of truth – so what difference would it make to add another to the tally? Maybe she doesn't want to know and, to be honest, she doesn't really need to know. But I still wonder, because I wonder what it would be like to have that sort of relationship with my mother. I wonder what she would say if I told her I'd had sex more than once, with more than one person, and sometimes with more than one person at a time. I have to wonder, because I don't know that the reaction would be entirely positive.

I wonder what the conversation would sound like. Would it be entirely in Chinese euphemisms, skirting around the point without actually making it? Would she talk over me, with continual interjections, or would she allow me to say my piece, albeit in Mandarin spliced together by a wayward English word or phrase? I wonder what it would have been like if I had been braver when I was younger, if I'd straight out asked my mother about this thing called sex.

At the same time, I'm not doing myself any favours by dwelling on it. I'm just glad to have this opportunity to talk back to my mother, to say all the things I wasn't able to say when I was younger, and all the things I don't think I'll be ever able to say to her in person. This is my way of being heard; by getting it all down on paper, I'm releasing all these things that have been left unsaid, allowing myself to name them on my own terms, to make them real.

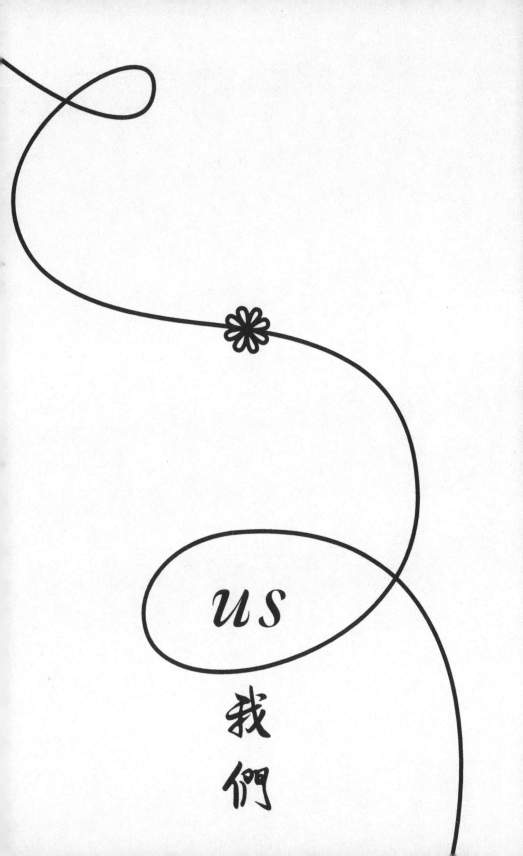

us

我們

6

Yellow Fever

I've always wanted to have sex with an Asian, reads a message on Tinder. I take a screenshot, blot out the person's profile picture and name, and send out an angry tweet.

Are you a nympho? Asian girls are nymphos, they always wanna bang, reads another message. A five-minute pause, as if this is an appropriate amount of time to wait before launching into—

Wanna fuck?

Even if I did want to before, I don't want to now, I think. I unmatch.

I first heard the term 'yellow fever' when I was in my early teens. I wasn't bothered by it at the time, and I didn't say anything while my friends, mainly the boys, teased each other about having it. This type of joking has led to the popularisation of this phrase – there are thirty-four separate entries on UrbanDictionary.com for 'yellow fever', some of which are extremely racist and sexist, all of which are written in a joking manner. It's difficult to pinpoint when this phrase became acceptable for mainstream use in this way, but it is clearly related to the belief that Asian people have 'yellow' skin.

The origins of attributing yellow skin to people of East Asian descent are hard to track. As historian and professor of foreign languages Michael Keevak notes in his book *Becoming Yellow: A Short History of Racial Thinking* (Princeton University Press, 2011):

> Trying to trace any straightforward development of the concept of yellowness is full of dead ends, because [...] like most other forms of racial stereotyping, it cannot be reduced to a simple chronology and was the product of often vague and confusing notions about physical difference, heritage, and ethnological specificity.[1]

Keevak argues that people of East Asian descent were not really known by a particular colour until Carl Linnaeus, a Swiss botanist who is responsible for binomial nomenclature (the system of naming organisms we use to this day) sorted humans into four categories – European, African, American, and Asian – and assigned them the seemingly arbitrary colours white, black, red, and yellow. In fact, Linnaeus used the Latin word 'luridus', which means sallow, lurid, wan – all of which connote weakness and sickliness – and, most importantly for his purposes, pale yellow.[2] Such a classification implies an inferiority, too – rarely do we consider weakness and sickness as positives. Indeed, Keevak also notes that there is 'something dangerous, exotic, and threatening about Asia that "yellow" [...] helped to reinforce.'[3] Such a mentality is given voice and action in the form of the yellow peril,* which was used successfully by the Western world throughout and after the colonial project to codify Asian people as Other, and therefore alien.

Sometimes, it feels trite to focus so heavily on a colour. But the connection between yellow and 'Asian' (or at least East Asian) is baked into popular culture in a way that is hard to escape. On the surface, yellow is a simple colour. It's a primary colour, the third colour of the rainbow, and like all colours it means different things to different people. For some, it conjures up the image of daffodils; for others, the Kraft cheese Singles wrapped in plastic that I devoured when I got home from school and were the staple of every primary school kid's lunchbox in the nineties and early aughts. For others still, it might be the doors of the Queensland Rail trains – ever slow to open, ever fast to close; the colour of the sun; a way of distinguishing which T2 boxes hold tea bags and which ones are full of loose-leaf tea. In colour psychology, the right yellow

---

* An idea spread throughout the Western world that people (read: immigrants) of East and South-East Asian descent were an existential threat to Western society. Basically, a fear that we were going to take all your jobs and seduce all your men and women.

can increase optimism, self-esteem, confidence, friendliness, creativity. However, the wrong yellow can result in feelings of fear, irrationality, and anxiety.

Yellow is also the colour of jaundice, of sickness. As a child, I never really saw yellow as a 'good' colour, as something bright or bold or beautiful. I knew it was somehow 'off', even if I didn't really know why. It's worth noting that yellow fever is also an 'acute viral haemorrhagic disease transmitted by infected mosquitoes',[4] according to the World Health Organization. The borrowing of a phrase that relates directly to a disease implies something dirty about me – my skin, my blood – that we are simply objects as opposed to fully formed people in our own right. I'm imagining these insects blanketing my face, crawling over my skin, siphoning my exotic, unclean blood and depositing it under the porcelain membranes white people call skin.

I resigned myself to having my skin tone described as yellow, or yellow-tinged. I learnt not to take offence, because I had to pick my battles; if I got angry every time I encountered a microaggression, I'd spend my whole life as a walking, talking ball of fire. In any case, my time was better spent on people who were willing to engage and listen, instead of those who just wanted to pick a fight. But the fact that my skin was 'yellow' crept into my life in other ways. In grade twelve, while we were trying on formal dresses, one of my Chinese friends told me, 'You shouldn't pick anything green because it brings out the yellow in your skin.' For nearly a decade, I didn't wear any green.

I've heard people dismiss claims of yellow fever as 'just a preference'; it's no different to having a preference for blondes or brunettes, they say (by comparison, hair can easily be dyed). These people desperately try to refute accusations of racism, lamenting the fact they can't escape the 'PC crew' interfering in their private lives. Pockets of Reddit and of the internet in general are filled with men who believe they are fully justified in only dating Asian women, and other people should leave them alone and let them do so. These men probably also believe they are God's gift to women, and that it is society's fault that they are not getting the amount of sex they think they deserve.

The way Asian women are depicted in porn certainly doesn't help when it comes to normalising the idea of having a 'preference for Asians'. Criticisms of the porn industry generally focus on the imbalance of power between men and women, but – as is the case in many spaces – lack the same depth of critical analysis when it comes to race. I am, and have always been, conflicted over the 'Asian' category on porn websites. I have spent a lot of time watching thin blonde or brunette white women with big boobs and perfectly manicured vaginas fucking immaculately structured white men who have cocks that look like they've been crafted from a mould. But I've never clicked into the Asian category, mainly because I know what's in store: the amorphous, non-specific 'Asian' woman or women fucking some white men. I have way too many experiences with men fetishising my race to ever find this sort of content arousing.

Representation is important, even in the porn industry, but poor representation can be worse than none at all. Denton Callander, from the Kirby Institute at the University of New South Wales, has conducted studies on race and racial bias on dating apps, and notes that 'where you do see actors of colour introduced [in porn], it's not on the same playing field as the white actors – race then becomes a feature of the porn storyline'.[5] It is not surprising to see this centring of white people as the norm in pornography; it's the norm in almost every other facet of Western society.

Some rebut this claim by pointing to Asa Akira as an example of an Asian porn actor who made a concerted decision to enter the industry. Even though she has now retired from starring in porn, she is still involved in the industry, releasing books, directing porn films of her own, and selling merchandise. She's a proudly outspoken feminist, believes prostitution should be legalised, and refused to do scenes that degraded Asian culture. But even she acknowledges the uniqueness of her situation, particularly that her parents are accepting of her porn career. 'I think they would obviously rather I do anything else,'[6] she says in an interview. However, she acknowledges that her parents were rebellious in their own ways, that 'their [own] parents weren't happy with what they were doing [...] So, I think that helps, because traditional Japanese parents would probably disown me.'[7]

Akira's fame doesn't mean the porn industry is absolved of its overwhelming whiteness, nor does it mean other actors of colour aren't exploited in the industry. Other porn actors of Asian descent have much less control over their work. Erika Nishimori, a part-time Japanese porn actor, acknowledges what she does on screen is solely for the benefit of her prospective audiences, while under the direction of other men. 'I play embarrassing gestures. It is acting to cry and be scared,' she says. 'I am making it so that men get excited. There are few such things in truth.'[8] It must be even more infuriating to know that these faked acts in porn inevitably spill out into people's desires in the real world.

At the party where I first met G, I don't remember how we struck up a conversation, but we did – there is photographic evidence. In the photograph, we are sitting on a white leather couch. We are both leaning back, and he has his arms crossed behind his head. Our faces are angled towards each other, and I am making a gesture with one hand and holding a red Solo cup in the other. I can't remember if I'm drunk at this point in time, but I'm most certainly on my way; I think the cup I'm holding contains a potent mix of Coke and four or five different kinds of alcohols that one of my friends prepared for me earlier. G looks content, if not amused. I don't know if this was part of the conversation on the couch, but I remember him saying, 'You're hot. Like an 8.5 out of 10. I added a point extra because you're Asian.'

It was the first time in a while that a boy told me he found me attractive. I knew the words sounded suspect – I knew there was something off about 'You're Asian so you're more attractive', but having been awkward and not-really-that-pretty for most of my life, I couldn't help but feel good that he found me hot. We made out shortly afterwards, fuelled by the almost-drunk bravery that only an unknown number of mixed drinks in a teenager can provide.

Years later, after M broke up with me, G and I caught up over Facebook Messenger. His current girlfriend was Asian, and all his ex-girlfriends had been, too. For some reason, the conversation eventually landed on my hair – I'd been dyeing it varying shades of red over the past few years – and he asked me what colour it was now. *I liked you better with black hair,* he replied.

The preoccupation with Asian women's attractiveness has also been leveraged in the food industry. In 2017, two white men (and DJs, no less), Ryan Vermaak and Fabio di Cosmo, opened a restaurant called Misohawni in Johannesburg, and were rightly and angrily called out by Asian women on the internet. Ming-Cheau Lin, a Taiwanese South African woman and food blogger, tweeted:

> A new 'Asian' restaurant opening in Joburg, owned by non Asians. It covers 3 different cultures: 1. ramen (Japanese), 2. poke (Hawaiian) & 3. Korean BBQ. As an Asian woman, I really hate the name. It might seem funny but when men say it while they sexually harass you it's not.

The name of this restaurant may have been a simple joke to these men, but being white men, they were blissfully unaware of the impacts this one term has had on Asian women since its introduction into popular culture. In the same year, Sarah Cattoor and Ryan Greening (yep, both white) changed the name of their West Des Moines restaurant from Me So Hungry to Eggs & Jam after criticism from the Asian community. In response to media enquiries at the time, they wrote, *The name came only from a love of the '90s and we had no intention to be offensive to other cultures,*[9] a reminder of the ease with which racial slurs can be normalised – even to the point where their true origins are obscured.

In a more recent example, as well as one that's closer to home, LingLing, a bar in Fortitude Valley in Brisbane, launched a food and drink menu with offerings such as 'Hardcore Asian Prawn', 'Love You Longtime', 'Sucki Sucki', and 'Mi So Horni'. An Instagram account, @rebrand_linglingsbne, skilfully and succinctly explained the historical origins of these disgusting names, and also urged people to sign a change.org petition, which ultimately received more than 8,000 signatures. It was only after all this that the menu changed – notably, however, without comment from the bar's owners.

The names of these drinks come from *Full Metal Jacket* (Warner Bros. Pictures, 1987), a film about the Vietnam War that was directed, produced, and co-written by Stanley Kubrick (a white man). In one scene, a Vietnamese woman, a sex worker – the very definition of servitude for the benefit of the white man – says, 'Me so horny. Me love you long time. Me sucky sucky',[10] as she tries to pick up an American soldier. These words were then mixed into a sample in 2 Live Crew's 'Me So Horny' two years later, and also by Sir Mix-a-lot in 'Baby Got Back' in 1992, and it is naive to think either of these artists was unaware of this quote's origin when their songs were released. Perpetuating depictions of Asian women like this reduces us into objects of consumption, vessels for disseminating what white men think Asian women should look and talk and act like; that is, a hypersexual being who is subject to the whims of the male gaze.

The persistence of such attitudes in society can have deadly repercussions for Asian women. In March 2021, a white man killed eight people across three massage parlours in Atlanta; six of these people were women of Asian descent. Afterwards, he told investigators he had a sex addiction, struggled with pornography and sex, and that his actions weren't racially motivated – a claim that sparked outrage throughout the Asian American community. Even though he was eventually charged and sentenced for these murders, Cherokee County District Attorney Shannon Wallace noted that he 'blamed the victims for his inability to control his impulses'.[11] By refusing to acknowledge or deal with the real issue at hand and placing the onus back on his victims, this white man, like many others, took centre stage in discussions that should have focused on Asian women and their hypersexualisation in Western societies.

The focus on the male gaze is also reflected in academia. Robin Zheng is a lecturer in Political Philosophy at the University of Glasgow, and examines issues associated with

148

ethics and structural injustice with a focus on gender, race, and social inequality. In the abstract for her paper 'Why Yellow Fever Isn't Flattering: A case against racial fetishes', Zheng notes much of the research conducted in this area focuses on those who have the 'fetish', as opposed to those who bear the consequences of being fetishised. I was stunned by this finding, but upon reflection it makes sense. Whiteness holds power everywhere. This also fits in with the language used to talk about this issue: white men have yellow fever, white men are the subjects of this affliction, while Asian women are their objects and don't even warrant a mention.

It is also important to note that while 'yellow fever' is commonly ascribed to white men who fetishise Asian women, it is something that still applies to all men. Young Black men have told me that banging an Asian has always been on their list; young Asian men have pestered me almost to the point of harassment about coming over to their place for sex. The stereotypes ascribed to Asian women can be internalised by anyone who encounters them, and there will always be a power imbalance if a man (no matter his race) believes himself to be in pursuit of a woman who he thinks will be docile, demure, and submissive. Indeed, Zheng also notes that 'individuals' racial fetishes *always* depend on racial stereotypes rather than pure aesthetic features',[12] effectively negating the 'just a preference' argument. Unless, of course, these men are willing to admit that they have a hard-on for the stereotyped image of a small, submissive Asian girl.

But Asian women – perhaps surprisingly to some – have

agency, too. It can be easy for our voices to get lost in these discussions, to get mired in the ever-present racism here, but we aren't just passive halves of our relationships; our desires are just as important as those of our partners. I know I have attributes that people would find attractive regardless of my race and its implications. The two long-term partners I've had so far have both been white, but our mutual attraction was based on each other's merits – or to be more specific, a love for reading, a wicked sense of humour, and a cringe-worthy obsession with puns and dad jokes. Of course, I've had my concerns; it would have been silly not to be at least a little wary of the reasons behind their attraction to me, but over time I grew to know them as individuals with their own complexities and nuances, as I'm sure they did with me.

The nature of whiteness combined with the societal hierarchy of the Western world has allowed white men to occupy positions of power. They are rarely required to account for or explain any of their problematic behaviours, meaning shitty white men are present everywhere, including academia, where they proffer uninformed and incorrect opinions under the guise of rationality. Stephen Kershnar, a 'distinguished teaching professor in the philosophy department at the State University of New York at Fredonia and an attorney',[13] is one such man. In 2019, Kershnar published an academic paper in the *International Journal of Applied Philosophy* titled 'In Defense of Asian Romantic Preference'.

Just reading the title of this paper made me angry; this anger has not subsided with time. Even if he was simply playing devil's advocate (a favourite pastime of white men), and had somehow trolled his way into an academic journal for shits and giggles, the paper puts forward the opinion that there's simply nothing wrong, unjust, or immoral when it comes to 'Asian romantic preference'. This 'research' then allows men – particularly white men – who read Kershnar's work to use it as 'proof' when defending their right to only date (or fuck) Asian women. This burgeoning obsession with the rational, with collecting concrete 'evidence' to throw in the face of women's lived experiences, which are full of emotion and therefore not worthy of consideration, is yet another way of invalidating and silencing women – and, in particular, women of colour.

If I wasn't writing this book, I wouldn't have given Kershnar's paper the light of day; I would have had my moment of outrage like everyone else and moved on. But Kershnar's work is truly dangerous. Providing yet another basis for racist white men to declare 'I'm not racist!' is increasingly damaging, especially in our current political climate. Even his reaction to 'yellow fever' is tinged with contempt. In the footnotes, he writes:

> Note that some people might find the term 'yellow fever' offensive. If the reader finds it offensive, please treat the above usage of it in this paper with implicit scare quotes to indicate that the elliptical use of the word to refer to a family

of attitudes [...] To avoid offense, I have substituted 'Asian romantic preference' for 'yellow fever'.[14]

For thirteen pages, Kershnar uses a bunch of jargon and deliberately manipulates syntax to make his argument sound more impressive than it is. The gist of his paper is this: white men should be absolved of moral guilt if they are only attracted to 'Asian' women. He does so by invalidating Asian women's lived experiences with so-called rationality, deliberately referencing Robin Zheng's work and the voices of the women she champions. Kershnar's argument stinks of a 'what about me' attitude prevalent in dominant groups who are not used to marginalised people pushing to have their voices heard, and feel that this can only result in their own silencing. As many people across social media have stated, *when you're accustomed to privilege, equality feels like oppression*. His use of language belies how he feels about women in general; he talks of women as 'competitors', as if women are dating like they are on a real-life version of *The Bachelor*, amassing in groups and pining after a finite number of eligible men, as if men are all women can think about.

Kershnar then argues that 'even if Asian romantic preference harms Asian women in some way, if the benefit outweighs the cost, the harm is not morally problematic'.[15] Such benefits, he claims, might include increased attention (women, he argues, put a lot of effort into looking attractive, and so welcome such attention), or a long-lasting and fulfilling marriage – never mind that many people my age aren't necessarily looking to get married, and being in a healthy relationship is literally the bare *fucking* minimum. This argument is easy to make when you aren't part of the group that is being harmed. This isn't the trolley problem – no 'greater good' comes of deeming this behaviour acceptable. Kershnar, men like him, and men who share his beliefs are only interested in one thing: maintaining white supremacy.

I'm re-reading *Growing Up Asian in Australia* (Black Inc., 2008), a collection of work by Asian Australians published when I was fourteen. I didn't know about the collection until I was much older, but reading it many years after its release still makes me feel a little less alone. In her piece for the anthology, 'How to Be Japanese', young adult and children's author Leanne Hall writes, 'there's something seductive in acting out a stereotype; life would be simpler if I only had to exist in one dimension'.[16] I find myself agreeing with this idea; things are much easier when you're not constantly wrestling with your identity and how that identity is perceived by the wider world.

Hall's words remind me of a boy in high school who said he was learning Korean because he wanted to meet Korean girls. 'They're the hottest of all the Asian girls,' he declared one day, out of the blue. He ended up dating my friend who told me not to wear green, but I don't think he fulfilled his dream of going to Korea to pick up. It's upsetting and disconcerting that there are plenty of men like this, men who think that their ticket to a hot Asian girl lies simply in a language course on Duolingo.

'I live in perpetual fear that I'll get caught out by a serial Asian fetishist. I snoop through photo albums to find out if lovers have dated many Asian women before me,'[17] Hall also writes. Nearly a decade and a half on, these problems haven't changed – we're just stalking people's Facebook photos and Instagram accounts. It's one of those fears that lingers in the background, one of those fears I have trouble voicing to my friends, because I don't want to be labelled as paranoid, or as the person who always makes everything about race. But I have to be hyperaware. Letting my guard down is not an option.

I understand why some women buy into the 'Oriental flower' stereotype – life would be so much easier – and there are times when I've been tempted to lean into it. It wouldn't be hard; I can be quiet and demure, and it's also much easier to be around other people if you don't challenge their expectations. But I know if I did this, I'd always have a nagging feeling in the back of my head, asking myself if I was causing more harm than good, if I was being too selfish. Would I be making life harder for the next generation of young Asian Australian women?

In my research into stereotypes attributed to Asian women, Sheridan Prasso's work has shown up again and again. Prasso is, according to her website, 'an award-winning writer, editor, and Asia specialist',[18] with bylines in publications like *The New York Times* and *The New Yorker*. She's lived in China and Hong Kong, and has been lauded by Hong Kong's *South China Morning Post*. While Prasso's credentials are impressive, it is jarring that a white woman has written a book called *The Asian Mystique: Dragon ladies, geisha girls, and our fantasies of the exotic Orient*. In an interview with *Asia Society*, she explains that in her research for the book, she uncovered a number of different stereotypes ascribed to Asian people in Western culture throughout history, many of which still continue today. She notes, 'I think that if I were Asian myself I might feel too angry [...] But as a non-Asian journalist with an anthropological background, I am able to write about them with a more objective eye.'[19]

Her specific mention of her background in anthropology makes me feel uncomfortable, especially as anthropology is commonly defined as the science of human beings, or, as the anthropology department at UC Davis posits, 'the systematic study of humanity'.[20] Prasso's intent may be sound – even 'good' – but her comments reinforce an implication of objectivity and, therefore, authority on the part of the white woman. At the same time, they also imply that Asian women's subjectivity and emotional responses to the topics at hand make them unreliable. This power imbalance echoes that of male objectivity and rationality against female subjectivity and irrationality.

An anthropological approach to the exotification of Asian women may be useful for some, and perhaps more so in an academic context, but there are few instances in which it helps Asian women navigate the everyday reality of seeing these stereotypes play out on their bodies. Such an approach does not provide meaningful answers for questions like *How do I talk to someone who is trying to tell me that his thing for Asian women is okay? Is it even worth arguing with them? How do I deal with the anxiety that comes with thinking men only like me because of my race? When is it safe for me to tell someone to fuck off if I think they're harassing me? Is it fair for me to ask my partner to stand up for me when things like this happen because I am so sick of having to deal with it on my own?*

Doing this extra emotional work while navigating dating – and, let's be honest, just *being* – in the twenty-first century is draining, and it makes it even more frustrating that in Australia we seem to be incapable of confronting these issues head-on. There have been relatively few discussions and articles written about 'yellow fever' in this country, especially compared to the prevalence of similar discussions in the United States. When articles are published, there might be a spike in initial hype, but it dies down relatively quickly, and there's no further discussion as to the reasons behind such attitudes, or what can be done to combat them or prevent them from occurring in the first place. There's no definitive answer for why this occurs, and I don't think it's because we're sick of hearing about it. Maybe it's because we're not shouting loud enough. The term 'Asian American' was coined and has been used extensively by activists for at least fifty years, and Asian American studies courses are available at many colleges and universities in the United States. However, there are very few comparable courses in Australia – the Asian studies courses here don't focus on the Asian Australian community as much as Australia's political and economic relationship with Asia or specific Asian countries.

It shouldn't always be on us, though. This issue is bigger than just our community, and likely has something to do with Australia's self-proclaimed multiculturalism, a term behind which casual racism can be easily hidden. But maybe this country isn't ready to face the fact we're not as much of the 'land of the fair go' as we think ourselves to be.

Hey Australian friends, just wanted to get your thoughts on relationships between Asian women and non-Asian men. Happy for you to DM me if you're uncomfortable chatting or commenting in public.

I posted this on Twitter and Facebook one night, because I wanted to know what other people thought about 'yellow fever'. I wanted their general thoughts, but I was also searching for opinions on the 'preference' argument regarding men who only dated Asian* women, and comments that had been directed at Asian Australians with non-Asian partners. I deliberately kept it vague – I wanted to see how people would interpret the question and what assumptions they may (or may not) have made along the way.

Some people, mostly strangers, took the post as an opportunity to tell me how they'd lived in <insert Asian country

---

* It is, again, important to note that in Australia 'Asian' usually means East Asian; that is, people from China, Japan, and Korea, as well as those from South-East Asia who have lighter complexions (think Vietnam, Singapore, Thailand). I know South Asian and South-East Asian men and women who have darker skin encounter a different kind of colourism and fetishism, and it gets even more complicated when people are from mixed Asian backgrounds.

here> for an extended period of time, and how that apparently gave them the knowledge (and the presumed right) to tell me how I should feel about white men who fetishise Asian women. Such men separate themselves into two main categories: 'not all white men' – that is, *I've been to <Asian country> so many times and loved the food and absorbed the culture and I respect the women so I should be allowed to date them* – and men who believe their 'preferences' aren't racist because they lived and worked in an Asian country for an unspecified number of years, which means they truly understand what it's like to be a woman from that country.

Some believed it was no big deal, and justified it in other strange, but no less racist, ways. One man commented, *it's all about the food for me. Can't stand western food any more [...] People are people. There might be something in it from an ecological viewpoint. Hybrid diversity leads to stronger genetics.* There's almost too much here – the minimisation of Asian cultures so it's 'all about the food', the insinuation of the belief that racial bias doesn't exist and 'people should just be people', and, finally, the casual attitude regarding eugenics.

There were people who decided that if I'd been getting unwarranted attention from white men, it must have been my fault – I must have been asking for it. *Let me ask you first, do you go for white men more?* asked someone through Instagram DM. This, of course, completely disregards the fact that I live in a Western country, so there are simply more white dudes around and, surprisingly, some of them aren't complete dickheads.

The most interesting set of answers, however, came from white women. I found the Venn diagram of white women who had heard of the term and *thought nothing of it until you pointed it out* both disheartening and shocking. There were instances of white women who said they had Asian friends who had mentioned it in passing but they *hadn't thought it was that big of a deal* until they started reading the comments from other Asian women on the same Facebook thread. I knew there would be some degree of ignorance, as there always is when it comes to issues outside your own purview, but the blindness to this was astounding.

And of course, I got stories from Asian women – friends and strangers alike. There was the woman who was told her boyfriend was only with her because she was Asian, the man who told a young Asian woman he liked Asian chicks because they're submissive, the in-laws who made jokes about marrying an Asian woman so you can tell her what to do and she'll do it – no questions asked. It's comforting and disconcerting that so many of us have had the same experiences. There's a camaraderie here, built on the knowledge that we are not alone, that we have all had to deal with the same comments (whether they had been made jokingly or otherwise). It's hard to describe how it feels to be in those situations to people who haven't and won't ever experience them, to explain the tension between feeling fearful and angry but also knowing you can't go too overboard with your reactions, to have all of this run through your head in a matter of seconds, because whoever you're talking to is expecting a response and you can't just stare at them in blank shock until they turn away.

It gets more complicated when we consider women of Eurasian descent. They may not have to deal with the attitudes foisted upon Asian women, but they have their own stereotypes to combat. In an article for *SBS* to complement an episode of *Insight* that focused on growing up mixed race, writer Yenée Saw notes, 'many Eurasian women feel an intense, hyper pressure to be beautiful',[21] and this is reinforced by the increasing use of Eurasian models in fashion and beauty campaigns. Their lighter skin is upheld in Asian countries where colourism is rampant, and in Western countries they are lauded for their unique features.

This is another type of fetishism – one also created and reinforced by colonialism and imperialist thought. I've lost count of the number of times I've been told that my white partner and I would have really cute babies – that 'halfies' would not only be adorable, but would also grow up to be extremely attractive. It's one more thing I have to consider if I ever decide to have children: how will that affect their self-perception and self-esteem, and will I be able to guide them through a form of fetishising and stereotyping I've never experienced myself?

The stereotypes associated with the petite, promiscuous Asian woman aren't just limited to the domain of white men – white women have been socialised to think and believe them too. In US comedian Amy Schumer's set 'Mostly Sexy Stuff', she implies that Asian women will always have an advantage when it comes to attracting men, thanks in special part to their small vaginas. The anxiety some white women feel over other women's vaginas is not just absurd, but also strongly rooted in racism. If you're genuinely afraid that your partner will leave you because your vagina isn't small or tight enough, maybe the issue isn't Asian women – maybe it's you, your partner, or both of you.

The perception that Asian women have tighter vaginas, and therefore are more pleasurable to have sex with, is incorrect, and yet wildly pervasive. In an article for *Healthline*, Nian Hu, a writer and former columnist for *The Harvard Crimson*, interviews young Asian American women about their experiences with this myth. She reveals that it's an idea 'tossed around by quite a few people and in pop culture',[22] and that it is, for some, directly related to desirability. This mentality can be incredibly damaging, especially when it is being absorbed by young teenagers; as one anonymous woman writes for the website *Everyday Feminism*, 'I was thirteen when I learned that my tight Asian pussy was in high demand – and it shaped a perception of myself as a receptacle in sex, not an agent, as a means to an end (ejaculation).'[23]

There's no documented origin for this belief, but it is suspected to stem from – what else – colonialism. The mistreatment and forced prostitution of women in Thailand, South Korea, the Philippines, and Vietnam during American imperial invasions led many to believe Asian women were desirable because they were small and petite – including their vaginas. The perpetuation of such stereotypes, especially when sugar-coated in comedy, is particularly dangerous for young Asian women. It's so much easier to internalise these messages at this point in their lives, particularly as it is a time when many of them are also trying to figure out where they fit in the world at large. And when 'feminist' comedians like Schumer disseminate such values on a global stage, it's not hard to see how untruths can spread throughout the wider community. White women can be just as culpable as white men when it comes to the fetishising of Asian women. Their methods may not be as brusque, but they are harmful all the same.

Artist and photographer Yushi Li, who describes herself as a 'Chinese woman who is taking pictures of naked photos of men in the UK',[24] is reimagining relationships between white men and Asian women on a global scale. Her first series, *My Tinder Boys*, features fifteen men in their kitchens. Li used Tinder to source her subjects, and her choice to take these photographs in the kitchen, a site of domesticity traditionally attributed to women, adds another layer of subversion to her work. *Your Reservation Is Confirmed* takes this concept a step further – Li appears in these images fully clothed, while the men remain naked. However, unlike naked women in similar works, the men in Li's photographs are not overtly sexualised; instead, they perform everyday tasks like watering the plants, walking up the stairs, and doing yoga. In an interview with journalist Charlotte Jansen for *Elephant Magazine*, Li says:

by photographing those male nudes, especially with myself in the same scenes, I try to use the contrast between me the clothed Chinese woman and naked Caucasian men to demonstrate my desire to return the Western gaze onto those men, and question the exoticisation and eroticisation of Asian women like me.[25]

Her work is uncomfortable for some – we are used to seeing naked women, but it is jarring to see similar images of naked men, especially white men. Li explains, 'The main reason most of my models are Caucasians is that I think of my work as a response to the infatuation for Asian women, who have been considered as docile, delicate and exotic objects of fascination in Western societies.'[26]

Li's work is unique; she is among the first to display images of naked men from and primarily for the gaze of (straight, Asian) women. This reclamation of bodily autonomy is sorely needed and long overdue. It's a small but significant step in the fight for Asian women to be seen as people instead of objects or symbols, to stop being defined solely by colour.

I've recently started to try and reclaim the word 'yellow', and I'm less afraid of using it as a descriptor when I'm making fun of myself. When I was younger, these sorts of jokes would be a kind of defence mechanism – I figured it'd be harder for other people to hurt or judge me if I got there first, and it also made it easier for me to absorb the blows that might come later – but nowadays, I realise such comments reveal more about others than they do about me. One of my friends once used the term 'yellow fellow' in casual conversation, and since then I've been trying to use it as much as possible, when appropriate. Sometimes it makes people feel uncomfortable – funny that being explicit about your race and the stereotypes associated with it tends to make white people shrink a little in their seats.

When it comes to a change that is a bit more tangible, I'm proud to say that I wear green now. I've worn green on dates and to work. No-one's ever commented on it bringing out the yellow in my skin.

I still worry about men's motivations, especially when it comes to dating – I wonder if they've swiped right on me just because I'm Asian, if they think I'll have a small vagina, if they'll automatically assume I'll be submissive in bed. I'd be foolish not to; it has the propensity to rear its ugly head at any time.

On a balmy February evening, I was getting ready for bed when a text message popped up on my phone.

Heyy. Asian chick?

Who the fuck is this? White dick?

Haha yeah. Chill out I didn't mean it in a racist way :

Of course not, I think.

Well, you can merrily fuck off then.

7

Race Traitor

In December 2011, Constance Wu, star of the television sitcom *Fresh off the Boat* (20th Century Fox Television, 2015–2020) and the film adaptation of *Crazy Rich Asians*, began dating Ben Hethcoat, a white actor. They broke up in early 2018, but not before Wu was submitted to intense criticism and backlash over her choice in men. In one example, as part of an article titled 'Asian Men Endure a Unique Type of Racism (and Why Asian Women Shouldn't Ignore It)', American writer Natalie Ng states that Wu's relationship with a white man 'only further perpetuates the false notion that Asian men have so many undesirable characteristics that not even our activists want to be with them'.[1]

Being a voice for Asian women in Western societies and dating a non-Asian man are not mutually exclusive – and let's be honest, many white men have a few undesirable characteristics of their own. Yes, advocacy should be as inclusive as possible, but the responsibility of advocating for Asian people does not solely lie with women. Asian men can't point to a problem and expect Asian women to make everything right for them, never mind the fact that one of the main goals of feminism should be to dismantle the Westernised, patriarchal structures that underpin toxic masculinities, a goal that would ultimately be beneficial for Asian men and women alike. In light of this, it seems counterintuitive for these same men to demand women fight for them within the framework of a system that is rigged against anyone who is not a straight white cis man.

Ng's piece was released a few months after a similar article called 'Dear Asian Women, I Am Calling You Out on This One' by Eliza Romero.[2] Romero claims it is a double standard for Asian women who have only dated white men to criticise other white men for having an 'Asian fetish'. She argues that Asian women – especially those with lighter skin – have more privilege than Asian men (presumably because white men find them more attractive, which is all kinds of messed up), and that Asian men are emasculated by Western media. These representations of men lead Asian women to develop a form of internalised racism and, consequently, an unwillingness to admit they have a 'white guy fetish'. I understand where Romero is coming from, but I disagree with her analysis. Claiming Asian women have more privilege than Asian men in white society places whiteness on a pedestal, and again frames fetishisation in a positive manner. This argument also treats Asian women as a monolith, and strips out the nuance needed in such a discussion. Romero conveniently disregards the fact that Asian men often seek out white women too, and yet they do not cop the same flak as Asian women when they date white men.

It's unnerving that these pieces are written by women, and that there are many more Asian women out there who are willing to denounce other Asian women for dating a white guy. Surely they should be the ones who most understand what it's like to be typecast based on their race or criticised for who they're dating?

Many rebutted Ng's article, including Austin Chavez, the author of an article titled 'On Interracial Dating, Toxic Asian Masculinity, and Feminist Agency'. After deconstructing Ng's points, he concludes by saying space should be made for Asian men to talk about masculinity and for Asian women to unpack their preferences, but 'if we are having these conversations to stroke the egos of Asian men, then I want no part of it'.[3] Chavez hits the nail on the head here – putting down and attacking others isn't constructive, and racism cannot and should not be combated using the tools of the patriarchy. Believe it or not, Asian women have agency over their relationships. And just as a white man in a relationship with an Asian woman should not be automatically accused of having 'yellow fever', Asian women should not automatically be accused of being race traitors – that is, having abandoned or betrayed their race – because they fall in love with someone who isn't also Asian.

As someone who's slept with and dated many white men, and someone currently in a relationship with a white man, the idea of the 'race traitor' is something I'm particularly attuned to. Even though it shouldn't matter, my first crush was on a Filipino boy, my first kiss was with a Vietnamese boy, and I've dated and slept with men of varying ethnicities. For what it's worth, non-white boys have broken up with me as many times as I have broken up with them, and I've been on dates with more non-white women than white women. But that's the point – it *shouldn't* matter, and I *shouldn't* have to prove that I'm the one in the 'wrong' here. Despite this history, it still probably won't have any effect on those who see my relationships and interactions with white men as proof that I've betrayed my race.

I don't remember what I tweeted to prompt this response, but a woman who has never met me in person and who knows nothing about me once sent me a tweet at two-thirty in the morning: *How can you advocate for the deterioration of white supremacy while literally in bed with the oppressor? The fact that you are still receptive to/seeking white men means that you're still upholding white supremacy and Eurocentric masculinity ideals.* I was taken aback by her overuse of academic language – I didn't know if it was because there were so many of these terms in one space that made them start to meld into one meaningless, obfuscating blob, or if it was because it was two-fucking-thirty and my brain wasn't fully switched on. Maybe it was a bit of both.

I'd seen prominent Asian American women be viciously attacked on Twitter for having white husbands or boyfriends, but I was just a normal person on the other side of the world. I found it interesting and upsetting and infuriating that an Asian woman was angry at me for even considering white men as potential partners – most of the attacks I'd seen in the past had come from Asian men, who were incensed at my audacity to sleep with or date whoever I want, regardless of their race. Sleep with too many people and I'm a slut; sleep with too few and I'm a prude. And now, according to this woman, sleeping with the wrong people means my vagina supports white supremacy.

My brain stumbled into a panic. None of my Australian friends were awake, so I scoured my Twitter feed for someone who might be. I ended up chatting to a Singaporean Chinese woman who lives in the UK – an acquaintance I'd interacted with briefly on Twitter on a few occasions, but someone I'd never met in person. She reassured me, validated my belief that this sort of ideology was bullshit, and let me know that it was okay to feel shitty about something as seemingly insignificant as a tweet. (She also told me to go back to sleep.) But halfway through our conversation, she made a point I hadn't really considered before: *I don't know how many people on Twitter have worked out that my girlfriend is white but I have NEVER gotten flack for dating her which just goes to show what people's priorities are.*

I followed her advice and went back to bed, but the thought still lingered when I woke up at a more appropriate time: *Am I a race traitor? Do I actually have a glut of internalised racism that I'm not aware of? Does dating or even casually sleeping* with white men mean I throw away all these aspects of my Malaysian Chinese identity?

I've never been the sort of person who loses themselves in their friends or partners. I have a personhood that's independent of my race and cultural background, a sense of humour and a moral compass that have been tuned as a result of myriad factors, including where I went to school, the people I associated with and still associate with, the social media accounts I follow, and the media I consume. Even though I know all this, I still second-guess myself; I feel like I'm being gaslighted by members of the very community who I thought would be on my side.

I'm not unattracted to Asian men, but I know I have preconceived notions about Chinese boys that I have been learning to shake, most of which stem from an offhand comment my mother made: '中國的男孩子, 特別是那些獨生子女, 都被寵壞了, 爸爸媽媽當做他們是小王子這樣, 他們要甚麼就給甚麼.' I don't know if it was confirmation bias, but after this comment, I started noticing that the Chinese boys I knew who were also only children did seem to be more selfish and stuck-up. I may have carried this bias with me into my dating life, where it has been exacerbated by some average dating experiences with Asian men.

I have, of course, also been on horrible dates with white men, but maybe the difference is that I don't necessarily expect as much from these dates. I get excited about dates with Asian men – and particularly men who speak Mandarin – because I assume an unspoken cultural kinship. I assume I won't have to explain filial piety, or how it feels to grow up torn between two cultures that accept and reject you simultaneously. I assume they'll get my cheesy Mandarin puns that I don't get to inflict on any of my monolingual English-speaking friends.

There is an internal conflict at play here, one I don't think I'll ever resolve. *Do I hold Asian men to a higher standard than I do white men?* I don't think so, but others may beg to differ. *Do I have a 'white man fetish'?* The very phrase makes me cringe. A Chinese Australian friend of mine once told me I had more confidence than her because I was dating a white guy. 'I fall apart around white men,' she said. 'I'm always trying to win their approval; it's fucked, I know.' She thinks Asian women who are dating white men have 'made it', like they've achieved some sort of social or cultural capital. She thinks white men are worth more than her. I didn't know what to say, or if anything I said would be of any genuine help to her.

I've only ever brought two of my partners to meet my parents – both of them were white. My sister's long-term partner is also white. Of course, my parents would prefer it if I brought home a Chinese boy, but I don't think they see my dating white men as an affront to my heritage or my culture. My parents may have misgivings about my partners' willingness to engage with my Chinese-ness, but at the end of the day, that's my problem and relates to how I want to live my life. I'm pretty sure they're probably just happy that I have a boyfriend at the ripe old age of twenty-nine – my biological clock is ticking, don't you know? But in our hyperreal, interconnected world, relationships aren't just scrutinised by immediate family and friends – they're also open to criticism from people on the internet, whether they be online friends or strangers from the other side of the world, like that woman who tweeted at me at two-thirty in the morning.

Twitter is also where I found Joshua Luna's comic *ReconciliAsian,* which blew up my feed a couple of years ago. The comic has two horizontal panels; the top panel is split in two, with an Asian man on the left-hand side, and an Asian woman on the right-hand side. To the left of each figure, Luna writes of the ways in which they have been hurt – for Asian men, 'systematic emasculation, desexualisation, erasure & dehumanisation'; for Asian women, 'systematic fetishisation, hypersexualisation, objectification & dehumanisation' – as well as the ways in which they have hurt each other. Luna argues that both 'sides' should be aim to be reconciliatory, but in the bottom panel he reveals that what actually occurs are confrontations filled with accusations and arguments. The comic ends with the same man and woman in the top panels pointing at each other and yelling, 'we choose retribution!'

I recognise the positive intent behind the comic, but under 'how we've hurt Asian men' and the drawing of the Asian woman, Luna writes, 'Complicity and/or participation in white supremacy against Asian men under the guise of racial preference.' I'm revisiting this comic for the purposes of this chapter, and rereading this phrase still makes me feel uncomfortable – it's so absolutist, and doesn't provide space for the nuances that are integral to discussions around this topic.

Luna received an overwhelming amount of critique over this work, and in response he amended his original post, where he acknowledged the misogyny and patriarchal pressures faced by Asian women within their own communities, and that they should not feel an obligation to date Asian men. He also specifically stated that he did not oppose interracial relationships, and that the original purpose of his work was to highlight the 'unique sources of acrimony between Asian men and women that are so rarely adequately addressed'.

Such recognition is a step in the right direction; these 'unique sources of acrimony' should be discussed, but the use of two equally sized panels placed adjacent to each other still implies equivalence, regardless of the artist's original intent. Patriarchal norms and toxic masculinity affect both Asian men and women, but they are demonstrably more harmful for women. All men benefit from the conception of Western patriarchy and are influenced by it, unconsciously or otherwise.

Take, for example, the way Asian men in Western societies buy into the Orientalist stereotype of Asian women: dainty, petite, polite, submissive. It must be hard not to, especially when it's a pervasive trope in much of Western popular culture. It's possible this desire to position themselves closer to whiteness may be the result of an act on the coloniser's part that postcolonial theorist and Harvard professor Homi Bhabha describes as colonial mimicry. 'Colonial mimicry is the desire for a reformed, recognizable Other,' he writes, *'as a subject of a difference that is almost the same, but not quite.'*[4] This idea of 'almost the same but not quite' leads to an ambivalence around and slippage of terminology, which allows for the adoption and normalisation of colonial language and ideology among the colonised. Bhabha also explains that these acts of mimicry simply serve to reinforce colonial power, as the subject will always be *'Almost the same but not white.'*[5]

Such aspiration towards whiteness is baked into the foundations of white colonial nation-states. Anne Anlin Cheng, an American psychoanalyst, builds upon Freud's ideas around mourning and melancholia to put forward a case for racial melancholia, 'a theoretical model of identity that provides a critical framework for analyzing the constitutive role that grief places in racial/ethnic subject formation'.[6] Before coming across Cheng's work, I'd never considered examining my experiences of racism through the lens of grief and grieving – partially because it seemed somewhat inappropriate, considering the benefits I reap by virtue of being a settler coloniser on unceded First Nations land. I'd never thought of racism as a function of grief or loss, or vice versa, possibly because these ideas seemed too gentle against the backdrop of the aggressive, violent racism I was used to. Racial melancholia provides a possible explanation for the never-ending pursuit of whiteness by people of colour in white societies. This melancholia is a kind of suffering whereby 'identity is imaginatively reinforced through the introjection of a lost, never-possible perfection', Cheng writes, 'an inarticulable loss that comes to inform the individual's sense of his or her own subjectivity'.[7]

This grief for what 'could have been' – *if only* they'd been white, *if only* they'd had access to the privileges that come with whiteness – compels some to aspire for acceptance in white communities. This is difficult for me to fully comprehend, because I've never wanted to be white. I know many Asian women my age harboured such desires when they were younger – looking in the mirror and wanting paler skin, blonde hair, and blue eyes – but I was always proud of my thick black hair, my language, my name. I understand why this phenomenon of wanting to be white existed (and probably still exists), and I can't imagine how frustrating and disconcerting it must have been to feel this way as a child.

This aspiration for acceptance in white communities is, ironically, used as a point of opposition against Asian women who date white men – they are, essentially, sleeping their way to the top of the racial ladder. Never mind that when – or if – they get there, they will still be seen as lesser than, simply by virtue of being a woman.

It is possible that the idea of a 'lost, never-possible perfection' affects men more than it does women, thanks to socialised concepts of Western masculinity; that is, some men may view proximity to whiteness as necessary for financial and social success. But it bears repeating that Asian men who date white women are not subject to the same amount of scrutiny. No-one accuses Asian men in such situations of sleeping their way to the top of the privilege pyramid.

*

I was lucky to have been gifted a love for and understanding of my cultural background that I held throughout my childhood and still hold to this day. Traditional Chinese superstitions and beliefs are embedded in my brain: I still feel uncomfortable when I see chopsticks stuck into a bowl, and I follow the Chinese zodiac with more interest than I've ever had for anything associated with star signs. I have a deep appreciation of and continual fascination for the Chinese language, and it is Mandarin that comes easiest to me when I am scared or worried or tipsy. These attributes and behaviours are an integral part of who I am as a human being, how I hold myself, how I understand the world.

I am, of course, not the perfect Chinese daughter. I could have been – I could be – as I know all the right things to say and do to meet my parents' expectations. But would this make me happy, or even content with my life? I definitely wouldn't be the person I am today, and I might even be estranged from my culture and my community. I understand the impetus for those who deliberately choose to date outside their race – an expectation to abide by strict rules can easily lead to resentment of those same rules. Maybe dating outside of a community that expects them to continue in this vein is a way to reclaim their freedom, their personhood.

Many people in the incel and sex tourism communities resent the advent of feminism for apparently empowering white women to be more independent and less 'easy to get in bed', and there are sections of the Asian community who are similarly dismayed by Asian women who identify as feminists. The narrative is this: Asian feminism is complicit in white supremacy, which is personified through the rise of Asian women dating white men. In doing so, Asian women are deliberately and maliciously contributing to the continued oppression of Asian men in Western societies.

I am continually surprised by the backlash against feminism in communities of colour – not the harmful infiltration of 'white feminism', where white women co-opt conversations and movements to suit their own agendas while dismissing the concerns of women of colour – but simply the idea of equity between women and men. This isn't something that only happens overseas or behind closed doors. As psychiatrist Tanveer Ahmed, then a White Ribbon ambassador, demonstrated in 2015, men who uphold patriarchal inequalities are all too willing to voice their opinions on women's equality to the public. In a piece for *The Australian,* Ahmed claimed that 'family violence within newly arrived ethnic groups is often related to the sudden dilution of traditional masculinity, leaving men lost and isolated, particularly as females enjoy greater autonomy and expectations'.[8] This idea of 'traditional masculinity' as not only the standard, but also an excuse for domestic violence, is abhorrent and should not have any place in our societies, let alone coming from the mouth of an ambassador for an organisation that purports to support women who have suffered domestic violence, quite often at the hands of their partners (who are statistically more likely to be men). This victim-blaming mentality is yet another way to convince women *they* are the problem, reinforcing these ideas in those who subscribe to these beliefs, and absolving abusive men of their actions.

Ahmed's specific use of the word 'females' is telling, especially as he uses 'men' as their direct counterpart. 'Female' is an adjective, not a noun – unless used in the context of livestock. I cringe, sometimes physically, when I hear it said out loud. The use of the term is reflective of a belief that our roles, and therefore our positions in society, have been predestined by our genitalia; our subservience is simply the natural way of things. Misogyny can be – and is – rife within Asian communities, a possible consequence of the patriarchal norms that have existed for centuries in many Asian countries. Consider the number of infant girls who were dumped, killed, or given up for adoption in China during the one-child policy, as well as the ostracisation of women who give birth to daughters in countries like India, Pakistan, China, and more. In many Asian cultures, lineage can only be passed down through men, and the patriarchy looms large in daily life.

For women raised in cultures with these beliefs, a partner who has a Western view on gender equality may be more appealing – even more so if they have been raised in Western societies where these views are the norm. I certainly wouldn't begrudge a woman the chance to break free from this sort of environment if they had the chance to do so, but here, again, we encounter a double bind: the trope of the subservient Asian woman is prevalent across many, if not most, communities, so it's almost impossible for Asian women to escape these views (thanks, colonialism). There's no 'right' or 'good' decision here, so maybe it comes down to this: Asian women might sometimes date white men because of reasons completely unrelated to race. Or maybe this: who Asian women decide to date, regardless of gender, might be because of reasons completely unrelated to race.

Some claim Asian women only date white men due to self-hatred and/or a deep-seated racism against those of their own race. Internalised racism is an important issue that needs to be tackled on personal and community-wide levels, but attacking Asian women who date white men is not the way to have this conversation. Punching down has never been an effective way of engaging people in considered, nuanced debate. As psychoanalyst Anne Anlin Cheng notes:

> Beneath the reductionist, threatening diagnosis of 'inferiority complex' or 'white preference' there runs a fraught network of ongoing psychical negotiation instigated and institutionalized by racism. The connection between subjectivity and social damage needs to be formulated in terms more complicated than either resigning colored people to the irrevocability of 'self-hatred' or denying racism's profound, lasting effects.[9]

Internalised racism affects everyone – it's baked into the foundations of our imperialist societies. We have a responsibility to interrogate these effects and to help each other undo the harm it has caused us, but slapping a label of 'internalised racism' or 'race traitor' on Asian women who date white men is an easy way out. It places the onus solely on the woman, flattens the experiences of Asian people in predominantly white societies, and does not contribute to any sort of healthy discussion regarding systemic and structural issues that perpetrate internalised racism throughout our communities.

I'm not saying that Asian men in Western societies don't have to combat unfair stereotypes of their own – they are commonly seen as socially awkward 'nerds', subservient, and sexually unattractive. These stereotypes continue to be perpetuated in popular culture – see Raj in *The Big Bang Theory* (Chuck Lorre Productions, 2007–2019) or the imaginatively named Chang in *Community* (Krasnoff/Foster Entertainment, 2009–2015). But it's important to note that Asian men are only seen in a negative light because of a society that has been long governed by the tenets of toxic masculinity; that is, to be a man is to be physically strong, buff, stoic, and to have the ability to 'pull girls'.

It is interesting to note that many white women claim they're simply 'not attracted' to Asian men. In 2011, sociologists Belinda Robnett and Cynthia Feliciano conducted a study on 6,070 dating profiles of straight people in the US, and discovered that more than 90 per cent of non-Asian women displayed behaviour that excluded Asian men.[10] Building on these findings, another American sociologist, Grace Kao, along with her colleagues, noted that compared to white, Black, and Hispanic men, Asian American men – both straight and gay – are far less likely to be in relationships despite their relative socioeconomic success, thanks to a steady diet of media that continues to desexualise and devalue Asian men.[11]

Asian men in gay communities are also the targets of sexual racism – younger Asian men are targeted and fetishised by older white men, termed 'rice queens' – while on the other side of the spectrum, there are men who openly state their refusal to date people of Asian descent. In the first episode of Grindr's video series *What the Flip?*, two gay men – one white, one Asian – swap dating profiles.[12] The white man expresses surprise at the comparative lack of interest the Asian man's profile receives, learns of the term 'rice queen' for the first time, and has to ask questions like 'Are you interested in Asians?' to get responses from matches. In an Australian context, journalist and filmmaker Santilla Chingaipe talked to Alexander Montgomery, a man of East Asian descent in her series *Date My Race*, which aired on SBS in 2017. Montgomery only dates white men, going so far as to say, 'to me white people are the epitome of class and the gold standard of desirability'.[13] It's disconcerting to hear this from someone who's supposed to be on 'our side', but it's also the reality of living in a world where white supremacy is so rampant that its values are internalised by those it seeks to hurt.

Even though things are starting to change in the media's representation of Asian men – see Simu Liu as a Marvel superhero in *Shang-Chi and the Legend of the Ten Rings* (Marvel

Studios, 2021), Steven Yeun's Oscar-nominated performance as a caring but flawed patriarch in *Minari* (Plan B Entertainment, 2020), and Ke Huy Quan as Alpha Waymond in *Everything Everywhere All at Once* – it's important not to forget the issue of Asian men being deemed 'less attractive' than other men. It must also be pointed out that the stereotype of the emasculated Asian man stems from Orientalist thought. In a discussion on the *Shoes Off* podcast, host and Malaysian Chinese Australian Jay Ooi delves into this topic with a number of academics, a psychologist, and another young Asian Australian man. Together, they deconstruct the reasons behind this stereotype, revealing that Asian men were initially demonised because they were a supposed threat to white men, and that Asian and Western communities prioritise different traits, leading to the perception that Asian men are lacking when it comes to the West's notion of masculinity. Interestingly, one of Ooi's guests, Dr Timothy Kazuo Steains, a lecturer in gender and culture at the University of Sydney, notes that:

Asian male masculinity is a really good example of an alternative form of masculinity [...] I think it's actually super-interesting and potentially feminist as well because there is a certain kind of benefit to not being read as an alpha male in that there's actually a really interesting space where some other kind of ideal can be forged.[14]

White masculinity is potentially dangerous for non-white men and women alike, and it will take time for alternative forms of masculinity to be more readily accepted. In the meantime, it's still unfair (and, at best, unconstructive) to blame Asian women who date outside of their race for these structural and systemic issues – it's not like everything would automatically change for the better if we all started dating people with the same cultural backgrounds.

Many of the men who consider women who date outside of their race to be 'traitors' will acknowledge the issues associated with the fetishisation of Asian women, but consider this 'attention' as better than no attention at all. Personally, I'd be quite happy to receive no attention if it meant men would stop fetishising me based on my race. Some Asian men consider this hypervisibility a type of privilege, and while I will readily admit that being East Asian affords me privileges in Western societies, especially in comparison to darker-skinned people of colour and First Nations people, the insistence that this also privileges Asian women over men is a gross misunderstanding of the repercussions of fetishisation. This idea that privilege (or oppression, as the case may be) can be graded on a sliding scale is also to the detriment of the community at large. It ignores the fact that women are and can be still marginalised within their own communities, even if Western society has primed others to see them as more desirable.

Just as many men were slow to believe women at the beginning of the #MeToo movement, Asian men with these views – by virtue of a lack of personal experience – are unable to fully grasp the gravity of the physical dangers that come with being an object of desire. This lack of understanding is, of course, exacerbated by stereotypes of Asian women that are perpetuated through Western media.

But as I've discussed previously, Asian men who date white women don't get the same treatment or the same level of public vitriol. I don't see articles calling out Asian men in such relationships, and I'd be willing to bet that, unlike some of the outspoken Asian women I follow on Twitter, they don't get strangers hurling death threats at them. In what can only be described as a hypocrisy of extraordinary proportions, these men are lauded by their peers for their ability to land a white woman. For example, Madalene Chu writes in an article for *SBS* that her Vietnamese Catholic partner Andrew would 'regularly get high-fived'[15] when he was dating a Caucasian girl, and stories like these are relatively commonplace. Surely if Asian women who date white men are perpetuating white supremacy, the opposite must also be true? This double standard points to the core of the issue: that many Asian men (and women, I'm beginning to learn, like the woman who messaged me angrily on Twitter) centre whiteness and aspire to those ideals for themselves, but also police the behaviour of others in their own community to prevent others from eclipsing their positions in the social hierarchy.

An example of this appears in a post on the 'Monash Love Letters' Facebook group, a place where people can anonymously submit love letters. It reads:

*Looking for a long term relationship with a local white
beautiful girl / serious relationship / not hook up or sugar baby
About me :*

*I'm a rich Chinese international student. 24 years old
straight man. Has a Porsche in Melbourne. Has a maserati in
China. My parents bought an apartment at South Yarra for
'oversea investment' years before, so I leave at South Yarra now.
Will buy a house at good suburb after I get PR. Im learning
accounting in Monash. Im a bit short. But I'm a nice man, I
think so. I will pay for all our dating, including international
traveling together.*

About you:

*Pretty white girl. Local. First language is English. 18 or 19
years old maybe. Younger might be illegal I guess . At least Cup
D. Taller than 170cm. Loyal, Virgin, submissive, be honest to
me, love me, adore me.*

*If we are in a relationship, you don't need to worry about
money problems. I will give you good life. But the only thing I
need to make sure is you love me, not love my money.*

This could have been written as a joke, or it could have been
real – it's hard to tell, and this very fact makes the whole post
dangerous and frightening. It objectifies women in a number
of ways and upholds an image of an extremely young, white,
pure, virginal woman as the ideal. It also implies that men like
this think enough money can get them anything, despite the
truth that no-one can buy themselves a place in the exclusive
club of whiteness. And even though the comments called him

out *hard*, there were no direct threats of violence. But let's flip this. Imagine if a rich Asian woman had written a similar post looking for a white man. I can only imagine the violent backlash and the inevitable death threats she would get.

I've been talking to my friends about this chapter while writing and researching it, and some of them have started sending me examples they've seen on the internet and tagging me in posts on Facebook. In one Reddit post, a white woman asks for advice regarding a conversation she had with her Asian boyfriend. She says, *he had a conversation with another Asian guy about how him dating me means that he 'made it [...] Asian guys view dating white women as a sign of success because Asian men are seen as less attractive and dating a white woman proves that they overcame that'.* Even though I disagree with this train of thought, I do sympathise with the Asian guy here, because I understand the ways in which whiteness and the patriarchy have contributed to this skewed perception of himself and the others around him. *To him, a white woman is some sort of proof of his success or masculinity because I 'could have dated a white guy instead',* she continues, before stating, *I told him that I thought the underlying assumptions behind his self-perception [...] and his perception of white women as intrinsically more desirable than women of other races are based in racism, and that it made me feel fetishised and extremely uncomfortable.*

I shuddered internally when I read this last sentence; I still feel a little shiver of something reading over it now. I understand that she may feel as if 'fetishised' is the right term to use here, but in this instance I'm uncomfortable with what I see as a co-opting of the term by white women in such conversations. 'Fetishisation', or 'being fetishised', means something very different – and much more dangerous – when used in the context of Asian women. White women, especially those who are raised in Western societies, don't grow up with the same messages as Asian women do – messages that tell us from an extremely young age that we are desired as a direct result of our race. Or as one man (also on Reddit) puts it:

> *I am only interested in the best: Asian women. Why is that? Could it be their fine skin and long silky hair? Could it be the fact that unlike white women, they remember what it's like to be a woman: to be docile and submissive and respectful to a man? Could it be their delicate, playful personalities?*

Or could it be because you're a little bit racist?

Being fetishised as a Chinese-presenting woman in Australia is to have racist insults and compliments thrown at you, often in the same breath; to be constantly questioning if someone just likes you because of your race. I'm always assessing my surroundings and the people I'm talking to, looking for signs in their behaviour and demeanour and language that might signal physical or psychical danger. This sort of unconscious emotional labour is a matter of safety and survival, to struggle to be seen as an individual in everyday life, let alone when dating, to constantly be on guard. Being fetishised isn't a 'perk' – if anything, it's made me hyperaware of my vulnerability, and the number of people who are willing to exploit that for personal gain. It's also not something that goes away if you start dating a white person.

In the previous chapter, I mentioned that I conducted an informal survey on people's perceptions of Asian women dating non-Asian men. Through this, I discovered that many people were unbothered by Asian women/white men couples, though some did admit biases placed upon them by their parents or society in general regarding mail-order brides and the like. Some wonder about the healthiness of the relationship if they see a much younger Asian woman with an older man, but don't think it's any of their business to intervene. In fact, this type of relationship is usually what people have in mind when I bring up relationships involving white men and Asian women. Most agree that it's more common to see white men dating Asian women than Asian men dating white women. When I mention the 'race traitor' phenomenon to my Asian friends, most of the Asian men I know have only heard snippets of it here and there, if at all, but most of the Asian women I've talked to know what I'm talking about straightaway.

For example, a friend told me she was once on a date with a white man in a Melbourne cafe when she noticed a young Asian man looking at her almost disapprovingly. He didn't say anything, but he didn't have to. I don't know how I'd react if this had happened to me. A part of me likes to think I would have confronted him and told him to mind his own business, but I know I would have probably just attempted a semi-threatening death stare. I am angry that two decades of socialisation and self-preservation have led to such inaction, but I also know I have bigger battles to fight.

I still struggle to wrap my head around the level of indignation, outrage, and hypocrisy shown by some Asian communities when it comes to Asian women who date white men. It is targeted harassment, as, like my Singaporean Chinese friend pointed out, it ignores relationships that don't fit the heterosexual norm, such as lesbian relationships, those that include trans men and women and non-binary people, as well as people in non-monogamous relationships. What if I'm in a committed relationship with two partners, one of whom is white and one of whom is Asian? I've casually dated women – white and non-white – throughout my relationship with my current partner, so how does that dynamic fit into all this, or *can* it even fit into all this?

The very concept of a 'race traitor' – at least, in the realm of dating – is bullshit. As Dr Jane Park, a senior lecturer of gender and culture studies at the University of Sydney, says on the *Shoes Off* podcast, 'I would deny the fact that any Asian woman who dates a white guy is a race traitor. If you do that, you're saying, all people who date outside their race are traitors.'[16] Just as I'm not any less a woman because my partner is a man, I'm not any less Chinese because my partner is white. I don't start wishing for blonde hair and blue eyes, just like

I don't forget the superstitions my parents taught me when I was young, or how to read or write or speak Mandarin. My engagement with my cultural background should not – and cannot – be measured by the people I choose to love or date or fuck.

8

An Oriental Flower

I've always been intrigued by the term 'Oriental', triggered in part by its use as a flavour in the Maggi noodle family. My parents would buy them in bulk when I was a kid, but wouldn't let us use any of the flavour sachets that came with them. '太鹹了, 吃下來, 身體不健康啦,' they said, when I asked why we didn't use them. At the same time, they didn't like to see anything go to waste, so our pantry turned into something of a safe haven for discarded chicken, beef, and Oriental Maggi noodle flavour sachets.

One day, when my parents were out, I decided I wanted to know what the Oriental flavouring tasted like. I thought I'd like it most out of the three available options because I knew, on some level, that I had some sort of kinship with it. Bright yellow packaging crinkled in my fingers as I ripped the noodle packet apart. The shiny silver seasoning packet was next, and as it tore open, I was greeted by a dark-yellow powder and a heady scent. Needless to say, I was disappointed when the noodles didn't taste Oriental at all. They just tasted like flavouring, with no discernible taste that distinguished it from any others. After I tried the other flavours, I decided the chicken flavour was my favourite. Truth be told, I didn't know what it should have tasted like anyway. I had a chat to a friend about it recently, and she couldn't really give me an answer other than '… racism?'

'The Orient' is an outdated term, though some from older generations may beg to differ. When people name their establishments Oriental Spoon or Thai Chinese Oriental Restaurant or Oriental Garnish, is it because they think the Orient conjures up images of exoticism and intrigue? Is it what men think I should taste like? These questions have no real or correct answers, but based on my experiences, and the experiences of other Asian women, I think the answer is a resounding *yes*.

The image of the Orient as a place of mystique and wonder plays into a number of stereotypes commonly attributed to Asian women – stereotypes that I was only peripherally aware of when I was younger. I might not have been able to put a label on them or even explain them with any clarity, but I knew they existed. *Asian girls are supposed to be quiet*, I was told – not just by my parents, but society in general. *Don't cause any mess, don't stir up any trouble.* Even from a young age, I knew I already fit in tidily with a number of stereotypes. I was a quiet child, an introvert by nature; I was branded a 'nerd' by a white boy in my class who my teachers had paired me with because they thought I'd 'be a good influence on him'; I played and excelled at the piano and another stringed instrument (the cello); I was good at and loved maths; I didn't like sport; my favourite place at school was the library. Other kids didn't really want to talk about the things I wanted to talk about, so I learnt to keep quiet, to be comfortable in my own company, and in the company of books.

After I finished school, I ventured out into the real world. It was bigger and louder than I'd anticipated, and I was expected to match this tune and tenor. I adapted, but in my own way. I learnt it was okay to swear – that some occasions even called for it, and that it wouldn't mean I'd end up leading a life of evil and debauchery. I learnt that being loud didn't mean I was taking up too much space or that I was taking up space meant for someone else, but I also learnt that silence and quietness was a power in and of itself. I stood up for myself in my relationships when I needed to, learning that my opinions were just as important and should be as valued as anyone else's.

But this didn't stop others from pushing their unconscious biases onto me. When I worked at Sizzler, a well-meaning manager, a middle-aged white woman, told me several times it was weird to hear me swearing – even though everyone else around me did it, and it was seen to be the normal way of talking to annoying, grumpy chefs. We once had a conversation about this while I was helping out in the dishwashing area, racking mugs, the clink of blue and orange keeping me company while I waited for food to appear in the window. She'd just heard me swear at the chef for screwing up an order.

'It doesn't seem right,' she said, when I'm sure she meant, 'Nice Asian girls like you aren't supposed to say bad words.' I didn't fit the stereotype. People weren't getting what they expected from the package they had ordered. It made them uncomfortable; it was weird for them, and they expected me to 'fix' myself, to change my behaviour to fit their expectations. I think it was stranger – not only in this instance, but in general – when I refused to do so.

I came across Edward Said's *Orientalism* for the first time at university, and his analysis of 'East' and 'West' has shaped my thinking ever since. Said argues 'the Orient' as we know it in the current vernacular is a solely Western construct, one that '[reiterates] European superiority over Oriental backwardness'.[1] This conception of the Orient generates a psychological imbalance of power between the coloniser and the colonised (or the Other) that continues to be reinforced to this day. Orientalist tropes are everywhere in modern society, even if we don't realise it – and even if we don't realise the latent damage they may be causing.

Reading Said's work was revolutionary; I'd never heard of or read anything that so comprehensively described what I had been experiencing my whole life. It was mind-blowing to have a name for it, to understand that Orientalism was a construct of Western imperialism, and to see the insidious ways it has infiltrated the West's understanding of 'the Orient'. As Said notes, 'because of Orientalism the Orient was not (and is not) a free subject of thought or action'.[2] But I was also angry that it had taken me so long – and that it was only because of an elective literature course I was taking at university – to learn of the name Said or the term 'Orientalism'.

The roots of Orientalism lie in the fact that Western countries conquered and civilised and shaped much of the culture present in 'the Orient'. Many Orientalist tropes persist in Western societies, in part because many of them tie in seamlessly with patriarchal and misogynist values. The advent of technology (in particular, the internet) has accelerated our collective ability to transfer knowledge across the world, which has also resulted in an acceleration in the dissemination of negative stereotypes. Said notes that 'one aspect of the electronic, postmodern world is that there has been a reinforcement of the stereotypes by which the Orient is viewed. Television, the films, and all the media's resources have forced information into more and more standardized moulds.'[3] He also discusses technology's impacts of Orientalism on the Near East and on perceptions of Islam, but these concepts can be applied when it comes to Western attitudes towards 'Asian' women.

One of the ways in which the internet has aided in the circulation of Orientalist tropes is, of course, through pornography. This visual aid for those who may harbour an 'Asian fetish' is more accessible than ever, even on the most basic of smartphones. There are also more opportunities for like-minded individuals to congregate online, whether it be on old-school forums, or their newer iterations like 4chan, Reddit, Twitter, and Facebook. This allows people who may never meet each other in real life to come together in spaces to support each other, even before we factor in the algorithms that force social media users into potentially dangerous echo chambers. These spaces make it easier than ever to exchange harmful views and reinforce negative stereotypes, and the chorus of supportive voices can make it even more difficult to find perspective in a world that is already far too polarised.

Such social media platforms – and the stereotypes held within – also have the ability to influence journalists and news reports. If media outlets report on these beliefs without fact-checking or seriously considering their ramifications on the wider public, it can give them credence, and potentially an even wider audience. Such effects are increasingly alarming, especially in this day and age when clicks are the measure of an article's success, and news is often delivered to the masses in short, snappy, clickbaity soundbites. If these stereotypes and their propagation don't affect your everyday life, it can be easy to ignore it all.

But I – we – don't have that luxury. I have to question people's motives. I have to consider if my appearance as a Chinese-presenting woman makes me more of a target for a potential rapist because he might think I'd be more willing to acquiesce to his demands or easier to overpower. I have to wonder if that white guy at work continues to talk over me in meetings because he thinks I'm naturally meek and quiet. And then I have to wonder how much of this can be attributed to my race, how much to my gender, and how much to the intersection between the two? I have to wonder if that acquaintance said that racist thing out of ignorance or out of genuine malice, and then consider how severe my reaction should be. Orientalism – or at least its effects – are *everywhere*, and I often don't have the mental or emotional capacity to explain these effects to people who aren't willing to engage with me on a meaningful level.

Generally Asian girls are a bit more submissive because of the traditional cultures, reads a comment by a woman who claims to be 'Asian', under a post on FetLife, in response to a white guy who is looking for an 'Asian' submissive. I cycle through a range of emotions – shock, anger, resignation. Surely an Asian woman would know what it's like for other people to judge them based purely on this one racist and misogynist stereotype? But the claws of whiteness run deep, and I don't know this woman's background or her experiences.

I didn't reply to this comment even though it annoyed me; sometimes – and I know that by doing this, I am playing into the stereotype of the 'Oriental flower' – it is just easier to keep my mouth shut. Like all problematic power structures, Orientalism can be internalised by those who are most negatively affected by it – it's another symptom of existing in a society where the dominant gaze is white, male, cis, and heterosexual.

Australia, for all its talk of multiculturalism, is still undeniably a country ruled by the white man and the Western gaze.

Australia's claim of multiculturalism is easily dismantled – the White Australia policy was abolished not so long ago, but in its place we have policies that demonise refugees and asylum seekers, and an attitude towards ethnic minorities where they are only seen for their economic and political value. This disparity between words and action means that in actuality multiculturalism is not what Australia is, but what Australia *has*. Multiculturalism provides Australians – more specifically, white Australian politicians who are keen to avoid being labelled as racist – with a sense of cultural and moral capital on a global stage, and it is this supposed moral superiority that allows the 'model minority' myth to flourish.

This myth originated in the United States and came into full force at the same time as the peak of the civil rights movements. It is predicated, in part, on the stereotype of the quiet, hardworking Asian, and was used as a tool of white supremacy to undermine and squash Black power and racial justice movements. As Bianca Mabute-Louie, an adjunct professor of ethnic studies at Laney College, notes, politicians at this time were telling the Black community, 'Asians have experienced racism in this country, but because of hard work, they've been able to pull themselves up out of racism by their bootstraps and have the American Dream, so why can't you?'[14]

This deliberate pitting of marginalised groups against each other to compete for white society's approval only serves to cement its power, while simultaneously denigrating those in the minority. Asian Australians, too, suffer from its effects; that is, the pressure from not only our parents, but also from white society at large, to get good grades, a good job, and be a good, useful citizen of Western society. While the label of the model minority has been foisted upon a range of ethnic groups throughout Australia's history – think of the Italian and Irish migrants who were vilified before being accepted into the fold (or successfully assimilated) – it's stuck most potently to the Asian community.

The pressure to adhere to the standards of the model minority myth is huge, unspoken, and often unexamined. The model minority myth perpetuates stereotypes about Asian Australians: we are all good at maths; we all have tiger parents who won't take anything less than an A, and so consequently all excel academically; we are all forced to learn a musical instrument from an impossibly young age; we are all studying to be lawyers or doctors or dentists or some other profession that will make us a lot of money; we are all meek and submissive – especially Asian women – and those of us out there who are supposedly domineering and seductive can ultimately be tamed; we are quiet, obedient; we don't complain; and we keep our heads out of trouble.

But the model minority myth is just that – a myth – because Asianness is not a monolith, and because Asia is much more than East Asia. The model minority myth teaches us that if we stay quiet, white people will, in the tradition of the never-ending cycle that is colonialism, eventually find another group to attack and demonise. Maybe this explains the change in my mum's behaviour depending on her environment and her circumstances – she could be scalding with her rebukes in Mandarin and in private before turning around, smiling sweetly, and accepting compliments about her children from her patients or other parents in English. She wanted to instil in her children a strong sense of culture, but that was, in some ways, incompatible with the public face she had to show in order to be accepted in Australian society.

There is a certain privilege in being lighter skinned, of being East Asian – a more acceptable kind of Asian. Even so, anti-Chinese sentiment seems to have swept through Australia at an alarming rate in the past few years. Surveys conducted by the Scanlon Foundation show that as of July 2022, 39 per cent of people have a negative view of Chinese people, a significant increase from the almost 10 per cent recorded in 2010.[5] The coronavirus pandemic hasn't helped. In November 2020, researchers from the Lowy Institute found almost one in five Chinese Australians had been threatened or physically attacked because of their ethnicity, while almost a third said they had been subject to offensive language and/or treatment as a result of their Chinese heritage.[6] The model minority myth doesn't provide any meaningful protection against true-blue racism. It's a reminder that our success must be limited; it must not eclipse or be at the expense of the white population. It will, at best, allow us a pat on the back. No more.

Doctor Helena Liu, a critical theorist at UTS's Business School, has studied the ways in which some Australians who self-identify as Chinese engage in what she describes as 'strategic self-Orientalism'.[7] Some of these actions are a result of necessity, born of a need to survive in an often hostile environment. Liu describes two main behaviours: mythtapping and mythkeeping. Mythtapping involves invoking Chinese culture in a way that presents the person as being imbued with certain characteristics and wisdoms, some of which may be useful for 'the West'. These characteristics include persistence, a collectivist view on society, and the ability to read non-verbal cues – for example, one participant in Liu's survey noted that she was able to survive through a period of organisational upheaval because of her inherently Chinese capacity for endurance (or, as she puts it, 忍耐). These traits, while useful, may simply provide more evidence for white Australia to weaponise the model minority myth. Mythtapping may also confirm to some that Chinese values are wholly conservative, thereby running the risk of affirming and furthering stereotypes associated with Chinese women, especially those that portray them to be 'oppressed, long-suffering and in need of colonial salvation'.[8]

Mythkeeping is, in some ways, an extension of mythtapping. Mythkeeping sees Chinese Australians place themselves in positions where they are, as the term suggests, seen to be 'keepers' of their culture. This can be in a 'mystical' sense, as the people who know the reasons behind specific superstitions or stories, or in a more practical sense – for example, being able to get their white colleagues the 'secret' menu at that Chinese restaurant because they know the right things to say to the waiter. These may be seemingly innocuous gestures, but such actions ultimately contribute to a form of commodified cultural exchange, of seeing the Chinese person as a means to an end by positioning them as the exotic, mysterious, yet approachable Other.

I have felt the tension attached to being both Other and Australian my entire life. As a child, I struggled to fit in, even though I went to a relatively 'multicultural' school. The only way I could do so was by being quiet and staying out of the way, which clashed with my desire to be seen as Australian by my white peers. Liu sums this up nicely by stating that while 'participants internalized the white gaze and saw themselves as the stable, homogenous Other, they could not tactically reconcile that with their desire to be seen as fully human'.[9] Such insidious and invisible internalisation is the result of physical and emotional violence doled out by the Western patriarchy: we are kept in line because we are told we have value, but that value only lies in our cultural connections, our knowledge, and the fact that the white men in power can declare their country to be 'multicultural'. Otherwise, we aren't worth much at all – just pretty little China dolls.

Sexual violence and the commodification of Asian women's bodies have direct links to Western imperialism in Asian countries. Colonising powers did not just stake claims over their land, but their people, too, and often under the guise of 'civilising' what Said termed as the 'non-European "primitive Other"'.[10] Such 'civilising' included the construction of railways and 'modern technologies' (all on the backs of non-white labour, of course), the introduction of education for all children, including girls, and the upending and restructuring of social and political structures to match those in the West.

It was with the United States' military interventions in Asia – in particular, South-East Asia – that the image of the 'easily fuckable' Asian woman reached its peak. During the Philippine-American War, in which the Philippines attempted to resist American colonisation, American soldiers described Filipino women as 'little brown fucking machines powered by rice',[11] and said they were able to buy 'a girl for the price of a burger'.[12] The Vietnam War was also a catalyst for the sex industry and the stereotype of the hypersexual, docile Asian woman. Many American soldiers deployed to Vietnam took advantage of Vietnamese women, and their so-called 'conquests' were subsequently relayed home through films and books. In addition to the damage done in Vietnam, American military bases in Thailand played host to tens of thousands of soldiers for the duration of the Vietnam War, creating a boom in the sex industry there, where women continue to be used and exploited.

There are similar stories from the Korean Peninsula. The South Korean government wanted to keep American troops in Korea after the Korean War, and so some South Korean women were stationed near American garrisons and forced to be 'comfort women'. Even though this term originated under the Gisaeng system of King Sejong's Joseon Dynasty in fifteenth-century Korea, its use became more widespread in the twentieth century, thanks to the growth of this practice in the Sino-Japanese War and throughout World War II.[13] Cho

Myung-ja, one of these former 'comfort women' who is now suing her government, recounted, 'to make sure we didn't pass on some disease to foreigners, we were tested twice a week, and if it looked abnormal, we would be locked up on the fourth floor, unlocking the door only at meal times'.[14] These women were treated like commodities not only by imperialist forces, but also by their own government; they were an offering of sorts – human sacrifices – from one country to another. This transactional use of Asian women's bodies did not end with the war, but was compounded and reinforced in its aftermath by the mainstream media's portrayals of Asian women as meek and hypersexualised.

This is best exemplified in an article in *Gentleman's Quarterly* by Tony Rivers called 'Oriental Girls', which describes 'the great western male fantasy' (the Asian woman) as such:

> Her face – round like a child's [...] eyes almond-shaped for mystery, black for suffering, wide-spaced for innocence, high cheek bones swelling like bruises, cherry lips [...] When you get home from another hard day on the planet, she comes into existence, removes your clothes, bathes you and walks naked on your back to relax you [...] She's fun you see, and so uncomplicated. She doesn't go to assertiveness-training classes, insist on being treated like a person, fret about career moves, wield her orgasm as a non-negotiable demand [...] She's there when you need shore leave from those angry feminist seas. She's a handy victim of love or a symbol of the rape of third world nations, a real trouper.[15]

The way Rivers equates physical features to the character traits of 'mystery', 'suffering', and 'innocence' that Asian women supposedly all have is stomach-churning, and his description of the 'Asian woman' is not really a description of a woman at all. My blood boils at the phrase 'she doesn't [...] insist on being treated like a person', which is, in essence, the crux of this disgusting passage. The literal objectification of the 'Oriental girl' for the benefit and comfort of the white man is seen as a positive, because the last thing a man needs is a woman who won't do what he wants her to do – a man who cannot control 'his woman' is not really a man at all.

Rivers's description of the Asian woman as a 'symbol of the rape of third world nations' not only reinforces his inability to see her as a living being, let alone a human, but is also indicative of his blatant disregard and disdain for these so-called 'third world nations'. He seems to be saying, in the way of twenty-first-century rape apologists, that they deserved it – what else did they think would happen? Rivers uses this phrase to demonstrate that these women will submit – if not because of their innate natures, then at least because of their learnt response of submission for the sake of survival. The glorification of a woman's body as a 'spoil of war', let alone its use to justify the objectification of a woman's body, is abhorrent – but that doesn't really matter, because aren't Asian women beautiful, and nice to fuck?

The most upsetting nature of this excerpt lies in the fact I know there are many white men who still subscribe to such stereotypes. As legal scholar Sunny Woan notes, 'The White conquest of Asia is "far from being 'a thing of the past' but is a lived experience of many".[16] This 'conquest' affects both the women who live in these countries as well as those in the diaspora. We may not be fighting a physical war against the West anymore, but the intergenerational and emotional impacts are still well and truly alive, and are manifest in and on Asian women's bodies.

The stereotypes that come with the label of the 'Oriental flower' also lie at the core of the white saviour complex; Said duly noted that 'in the writing of travelers and novelists: women are usually the creatures of a male power-fantasy'.[17] Men who view Asian women as submissive not only think that they have the power to control such women, but also that they are actually doing them a favour, 'saving' them from the destitute life they would have otherwise been leading. This sense of overwhelming entitlement can then be a precursor to physical and emotional violence.

In a post on the incels subreddit, one user writes that *in Thailand it's MUCH easier to find a non-hooker girl who is happy to be your girlfriend than it is back in the West*, before briefly detailing his experiences with Thai 'girls'. In response, someone comments, *this is gross but they still slept with him, right? It's kind of their own fault*. It's easier to blame someone else – especially someone who doesn't look or sound like you – than to take the time to thoroughly examine the power structures at play and their effects.

The white saviour complex is normalised in our collective consciousnesses. Think Matt Damon as William Garin, a European mercenary in the film *The Great Wall* (Legendary Pictures, 2016), who saves China after Commander Lin Mae falls in love with him; Tilda Swinton as the 'Ancient One' in *Doctor Strange* (Marvel Entertainment, 2016), who then passes on her knowledge to Doctor Strange (Benedict Cumberbatch) in order to save the world; Noah Ringer as the Avatar in *The Last Airbender* (Nickelodeon Movies, 2010); Scarlett Johansson as 'The Major' in *Ghost in the Shell* (Paramount Pictures, 2017). As Asian American television and film actor Constance Wu tweeted after the release of *The Great Wall*'s trailer, the idea that only white people can save the world is untrue – *Our heroes don't look like Matt Damon. They look like Malala. (Gandhi). Mandela. Your big sister when she stood up for you to those bullies that one time.* It's too easy for us to accept ideas like the white saviour complex while they are regularly splashed across our screens. Just as we cannot be what we cannot see, we internalise what we *do* see.

When I was younger, there was next to no representation of Asian women in the books I read or the television shows I was allowed to watch – let alone anyone like me, a child of immigrants who had grown up wedged between opposing cultures. This meant I unconsciously latched onto anything that even momentarily featured an Asian woman. I remember reading Arthur Golden's *Memoirs of a Geisha* (Vintage, 1999)

when I was twelve, marvelling at the novelty of being able to imagine myself as the protagonist. Even though the protagonist was Japanese and the book was written as a historical memoir, part of me was glad to just be reading about an Asian woman. It wasn't until I was sixteen or seventeen, and learning to read books more critically, that I realised it was hugely problematic to have a white man write about Japanese culture in such a way, and even more so when I discovered the that he had co-opted a real geisha (Mineko Iwasaki)'s life for the enjoyment and voyeurism of Western readers, not to mention his own acclaim.

As Kimito Akita, a professor of communications at the University of Central Florida, notes in 'Orientalism and the Binary of Fact and Fiction in *Memoirs of a Geisha*', 'Golden's devices present the Orient as a commodified Western object: a fiction of the West, by the West, and for the West, yet received by the West as reality.'[18] This idea of commodification is reinforced by the inherent authority Golden holds simply by being a white man. The fact that he's written a book also gives him an air of legitimacy – after all, only *good* books by *good* writers are published, right? Golden may have intended for his Orientalist work to be read by a white audience, but, thanks to decades of migration, his readers now also include women of the Asian diaspora, many of whom, like me, may have had few chances to engage with depictions of themselves (or others who look or sound like them). A book like this reinforces the meek 'Oriental flower' stereotype for both white Western readers and young Asian women, who may unconsciously internalise such depictions and consider them to be the norm. Much like the idea of 孝順 and filial piety, it's difficult to explain or to even begin to describe this process of internalisation to someone who's never experienced it, especially as so much of it happens incrementally, over years and years of conditioning, that sometimes it can only be noticed when something manages to break through this invisible, almost impenetrable, shell.

Akita also argues that Golden perpetuates:

> stereotypes about geisha as sexually submissive women who aspire to become mistresses, bathe with strange men, rest their necks on special pillows to maintain their hairstyles, play shamisen (musical instrument) made from virgin kittens, and wear facial powder made from a nightingale's droppings. These misrepresentations reinforce the idea of Japanese culture and geisha as exotic, backward, irrational, dirty, profane, promiscuous, bizarre, and enigmatic.[19]

Such tropes are replicated in other novels, such as Richard Mason's *The World of Suzie Wong* (Penguin, 1957), a story about a young British man who falls for Suzie Wong, a Chinese prostitute in Hong Kong. Like *Memoirs of a Geisha,* it was so well received that it was adapted for screen, theatre, and ballet. The success and popularity of these Orientalist narratives and stereotypes perpetuate images of Asian women as flat, two-dimensional figures, leading them to be further objectified and commodified for the Western gaze.

The musical *Miss Saigon* is a classic example of such objectification. Based on Italian composer Giacomo Puccini's *Madame Butterfly* (which is similarly Orientalist but set in Japan, not Vietnam, a telling sign that Asian countries are interchangeable to white men), with a book (the 'script' of a musical) by Claude-Michel Schönberg and Alain Boublil, and lyrics by Richard Maltby Junior (all white men, just in case you were wondering), it tells the story of a doomed romantic liaison between a Vietnamese woman, Kim, and an American soldier, Chris. The story does not end well for Kim – after falling in love, she has Chris's child, and is devastated when he does not return for her after the war is over. She eventually kills herself after realising he has an American wife, and that he will not take their child back to America with them. Kim is a sex worker, forced to work at various sleazy bars, and is also controlled and manipulated by a number of Vietnamese men. Chris is the only man who is kind to her – her white saviour – because Vietnamese women are all frail, meek, and in need of saving. Such a depiction also makes clear that the (white) Americans are 'good', and the Vietnamese 'bad'. Because Kim dies at the conclusion of the musical, Chris not only escapes being labelled as a villain for not wanting to give his biological child a better life, but he also garners sympathy from the audience by virtue of grieving an ex-lover. In this story, like in many others, the white man becomes the only subject worthy of empathy and concern. The white man prevails.

As many have mentioned, this story may well have happened during the Vietnam War – in fact, we know it did happen, and that the children of these liaisons were often seen as pariahs by the Vietnamese government. It is not necessarily the story itself that is problematic, but the way in which it is presented, and the ways in which it depicts Vietnamese women and American men. Perhaps even more grotesque is the marketing and paraphernalia surrounding it – in a review for *Vulture*, critic Jesse Green mentioned the bar was selling cocktails named 'mai sais' during the 2017 Broadway revival.[20]

The musical's lyrics are also disturbing in how deeply they reinforce Orientalist notions. The second song in the musical, 'The Heat Is On in Saigon', is set in a brothel, and features the following lyrics, sung by American men: 'One of these slits here will be Miss Saigon', 'We should get drunk and get laid', 'I'll buy you a girl', and 'the meat is cheap in Saigon'. Contrastingly, the lyrics written for the Vietnamese women revere the Americans. In 'The Movie in My Mind', Gigi, the eponymous Miss Saigon, sings, 'And in a strong GI's embrace/ Flee this life, flee this place', a couplet that is repeated by the bar girls later on. The Americans' disregard for these women's humanity is juxtaposed against the women's reverence for the white man, and these are just two examples from the thirty-eight songs that make up the musical.

Miss Saigon ran for ten years in the West End in London, and ten on Broadway. It is one of the top twenty longest running Broadway musicals in musical theatre history, has toured around the United Kingdom and United States, and has been (and continues to be) produced in theatres around the world. I love musicals. I love the combination of theatre and dance and music, how fucking clever the songs are, how the reprises and the themes all fit together oh-so-perfectly. I love how they can be used as instruments of social commentary, even change. But their appeal gives them a power that should be wielded carefully. Inappropriate lyrics can easily be overlooked if the music is catchy enough; just a glance through the last few years of popular music should make anyone take pause, but much can be inferred from comparisons of public reaction. I find it interesting that Robin Thicke's 2013 song 'Blurred Lines' incurred such swift and deserved backlash for lyrics that basically advocated for the violation of consent, but there has been so little, comparatively, against the lyrics in *Miss Saigon*. Perhaps it's because of the musical's long life span; modern audiences are always looking for something new to critique, and it's not worth the time and space to re-examine older works that may be just as, if not more, problematic than the latest shiny scandal. Perhaps it is because the musical taps into deep-seated stereotypes that primarily white audiences consider to be true. Or perhaps it is because white women's experiences are deemed more important than Vietnamese women's.

Video games also present inappropriate depictions of Asian women that are rarely questioned. I've been playing video games for over a decade and a half; it's a malleable form of escapism, one I can enjoy alone or with friends, and one where anything seems possible. At the same time, the presence of Asian women in these fantastical worlds is minimal at best – they are virtually non-existent in AAA games, and make scarce appearances in indie games.

A thorough search for Asian women in video games left me with a list that numbered fewer than ten, and some, like *Portal 2*'s Chell, are only heavily presumed to be of Asian descent. The girl character in *Pokémon*, a franchise originating in Japan, is whitewashed, presumably to appeal to a Western audience (though this has been improving in the latest *Pokémon* games), as are many of the women in fighting games like *Dead or Alive*. Even the quaint and beloved *Stardew Valley* doesn't have any characters that could be tentatively seen as 'Asian'.

And though the video game industry is well known for its oversexualised depictions of women, it's worse for Asian women, as the games that do have some form of Asian representation often combine it with a distinctly Orientalist flavour. In an article about Asian Americans and video game representation, Vietnamese American spoken-word artist and poet Thien-Bao Thuc Phi notes that 'Asian women remain restrained to several stereotypical roles [falling] in line with typical Western notions: mysterious, exotic, sensual – and partnered with any race of man except Asian', and are also indicative of the Orientalist notion of 'East as inherently feminine'.[21] Fighting games, which have a higher proportion of 'Asian women' – think *Dead or Alive, Street Fighter, Tekken, Mortal Kombat* – are a good example. There are quite a few Asian women fighters in *Mortal Kombat*, and most of them are clad in 'armour' that barely covers their disproportionate chest size. Their weapons always reflect their

Asianness – for example, Kitana's main weapons are two steel fans, and Jade wields a staff.

Some gamers seem more interested in playing an 'Asian woman' in a video game than focusing on the game itself. Posts on gaming forums include *Love Asian women but I don't ever remember kitana being Asian*, and another where a user asks *why does MK have no Asian females?* with one of the replies being *I'm not asian, but I would like to see some asian females in the game. (I kinda have a thing for them).* Sara Ishii, who has analysed representations of Chinese and Japanese video game characters on discussion forum threads, also notes that when users discuss the gender and race of a character, they often do so by employing disparaging (see: Orientalist) stereotypes.[22] On a *Dead or Alive* forum, one user imagines a backstory for Xian, a Chinese character, by commenting, *She's also a part time lazy-eyed masseuse who gives you happy ending massages. Luv you long time.* Even when I was gaming heavily, I would have never presumed to produce backstories for the characters in the games I was playing, let alone ones with such racist overtones: I was more focused on the game's actual story or beating the next big boss.

The escapism provided by video games makes it easy to ignore or even miss instances of stereotyping that may have been picked up more readily in a book or a film. I'm annoyed at myself for not recognising the severe racial imbalance sooner, especially as I did go through a brief obsession with *Mortal Kombat*. I'm angry that my personhood as an Asian woman has to be fought for separately when it comes to different forms of media. I'm angry that white men still wield an inordinate amount of control when it comes to portrayals of Asian women, which results in the continued dissemination of Orientalism and Orientalist tropes. I hope representation in this space improves; as Phi points out, 'we're not all straight white guys shelling out $60 a game [...] The game industry can't afford to neglect us forever.'[23]

Depictions of Asian women in media, particularly film and television, are improving – we have come a long way from the days of yellowface – and are even becoming normalised, but there is still a long way to go. I love action and superhero films, but Asian women are either not present or are often written to the 'Oriental flower' stereotype. My favourite character in *X-Men: Days of Future Past* (Marvel Entertainment, 2014) was Blink – not just because she had a bad-ass power, but because she was played by Fan Bingbing, a Chinese woman. Even then, she didn't get many lines, and played a very small part in the film's narrative arc.

In *Deadpool 2* (20th Century Fox, 2018), there's Yukio, though she only appears in a few scenes, and plays the role of a quiet, demure Japanese girl who is only spoken about in relation to her girlfriend, Negasonic Teenage Warhead. However, in Marvel's television series *Agents of S.H.I.E.L.D.*, which debuted in 2013 and was still airing when *Deadpool 2* was released in 2018, two of the main agents, May and Daisy, are Asian women – but they are not characterised any differently by virtue of their race. May is a strong fighter, and Daisy is the superhero Quake, and they are both given complex backstories and narrative arcs that do not fall into Orientalist stereotypes. Similarly, I was overwhelmed with emotion after only seeing the trailer for *Crazy Rich Asians*, and such movies, as well as shows like *Fresh off the Boat*, while flawed, are part of a wider movement that is rewriting the ways in which Asian women are presented in Western media.

Additionally, the rising number of Asian women who are writing their own stories filled with three-dimensional, nuanced depictions of Asian women gives me hope. I sobbed through Lulu Wang's 2019 film *The Farewell* (Ray Productions, 2019; better expressed in Chinese as 别告訴她), which not only features an all-Asian cast, but also dialogue in English and Mandarin Chinese. It depicts three generations of Chinese women, all of whom have their own lives and stories, which allows Wang to carefully and deftly examine the differences between the collectivist nature of Chinese communities and the individualism encouraged in American society (and, indeed, most Western societies).

In Australia, there are shows like *The Family Law* (Matchbox Pictures, 2016), which features a Chinese Australian family; *Homecoming Queens* (Generator Pictures, 2018), a series where one of its protagonists is an Asian woman; and *New Gold Mountain* (Goalpost Television, 2021), which tells the story of the often overlooked Chinese miners of the Victorian goldfields. These shows demonstrate how subtleties in culture can have a significant impact on perceptions and understandings of self.

Vietnamese Australian essayist, columnist, and critic Giselle Au-Nhien Nguyen's work gave me an idea of what it's like to be a queer Asian woman in Australia, and played a role in my own path to accepting my queer identity. Michele Lee's 2018 play *Going Down* was something of a revelation – I went to Melbourne specifically to see it – and watching Asian Australian women on stage talking about and engaging unapologetically with issues relating to sex gave me a degree of comfort.

All these factors have combined to give me the confidence to talk more freely about sex, and to also worry less about what others might think of an Asian woman who is open about the strange things she likes in bed.

Such advances, however, are not necessarily reciprocated through society at large. It's been disturbing to learn of men who go to Thailand, Vietnam, the Philippines, and other Asian countries because the women there are more willing to have sex with them. As one commenter on the incels subreddit advises, *get out of the West and it's 100x easier to get women.* David Bond (otherwise known as Steven Mapel) sells travel guides and private videos on how to pick up Asian women based on his travels through Asia, but declares himself 'a single guy who likes Asian girls, who also likes to record his life'.[24] His use of the word 'girl' is infantilising in and of itself, even without the qualifier of 'Asian'. In any case, his materials, and those like them, feed the idea of the submissive Oriental flower trope, which continues to flourish to this day.

Men like Bond are fuelled by toxic masculinity, and many like him boast about their 'conquests', and run relatively successful websites where they sell tips and guides to sex tourism in South-East Asian countries. Asian women's bodies are again being commodified, not only for the psychological benefit of satisfying the Western man's masculinity, but also for their financial gain. This combination of arrogance and privilege – the assumption that they can readily obtain sex as if it is an object stored on a shelf at their local Coles – is sickening, and yet still not difficult to believe. After all, it's how women in general have been treated and portrayed throughout modern history, and as they say – old habits die hard.

Legal scholar and law professor Sumi Cho notes that in America, 'Asian Pacific women are particularly valued in a sexist society because they provide the antidote to visions of liberated career women who challenge the objectification of women.'[25] This dichotomy between the Western, 'liberated' woman and the Asian, 'traditional' woman means the latter are seen to be more desirable – if only for their pliability. The Asian women who still live in Asia who have internalised white supremacy, who believe proximity to whiteness is equivalent to an elevation in class or status, are then prime targets for sexist white men. Add to that the image of the docile, thin Asian woman with a small vagina, and many of these men believe they have hit the jackpot.

Interestingly, Tony Rivers – he of the awful 1990 article in *Gentleman's Quarterly* – had some thoughts on this too, noting, 'The stereotype of the Oriental girl is the greatest shared sexual fantasy among western men.'[26] Here is, again, the use of the word 'girl', as if refusing to acknowledge these women as women with agency will make them more amenable to men's wants and needs. This turn of phrase also emphasises the power dynamic between these two people: the West and the East, the older and the younger, the civilised and the uncivilised, the leader and the follower.

Being desired based purely on my race and what that implies during and for sex is something I always carry with me, but this isn't something I can readily talk about with any of my white friends. They may be feminists, and they may understand that this behaviour and the attitudes that underpin it are awful and grotesque, but many are still dismissive of the severity at which it occurs. 'I'm sure you're imagining it' and 'I think you're making a bigger deal out of it than it really is' are some of the refrains I've heard from well-meaning friends. This defensiveness and these attempts to 'explain away' their peers' behaviour may not be actively harmful, but minimising problematic behaviour normalises it (and, at worst, invalidates it) and keeps us from starting constructive dialogue around it.

In her paper, critical theorist Dr Helena Liu notes that some of her subjects use mythtapping and mythkeeping as a form of resistance against such Orientalist attitudes, to reframe, redefine, and reclaim what it means to be Chinese in Australia. In some ways, this is encouraging, but the onus and the emotional labour should not always lie with us. Resistance is hard. It is draining. It involves speaking up, speaking out, and fighting the same battles over and over in the hope of incremental change.

We have, for far too long, been seen as quiet, submissive, unwilling to speak out or stir up trouble – never mind the reasons behind such silence. But now, the tide is slowly turning. There is such inherent power, to say nothing of the sense of validation, that comes with young Asian women seeing themselves reflected in the media they consume and the books they read, not least because it allows them to feel like they belong in this world that is so often dominated by the Western gaze. This cannot be replicated anywhere else, by anyone else.

These changes aren't just for the benefit of our communities – they're good for society as a whole. Our Black and brown and Indigenous sisters and brothers have always been there for us, but it's now time for everyone else to step up.

If you're reading this and you're white, there's so much you can and should do; the stereotypes I've discussed here won't magically go away on their own. This might be as simple as speaking up when you hear someone at work assume that your Asian co-worker will automatically follow orders. It might be allowing yourself to be more open to and seeking out people with life experiences that are different to your own, or that you recognise and work on your biases when it comes to discussions around race and perceptions of Chinese and 'Asian' people at large.

And finally, to all of my yellow fellows: it's okay to be

exhausted, to feel like nothing will ever change, and it's okay to be angry, to take time for yourself, to recharge, to remember who and what brings you joy. I said this at the beginning of the book, and I'll say it here again: you are not alone.

Acknowledgements

My deepest gratitude to the following:

Alice Grundy: for that lovely chat so many years ago in Sydney, for pushing me to get my thoughts out of my head and onto paper, and for encouraging me through the early years of this project. This wouldn't have happened without you.

Fiona Wright: you're an absolute genius; your gentle but firm guidance was exactly what I needed. You helped me figure out the structure of the book, which is when it really started to come together – I cannot thank you enough for your support.

Madonna Duffy, Felicity Dunning, Ian See, and the amazing team at UQP: you've all been so patient and kind and generous with your time and knowledge. Special thanks to Felicity for dealing with all of my early morning and late night texts about permissions and referencing!

Jenna Lee: for my beautiful cover, and bearing with my nit-picking and minor changes. Daniel Kuek: for designing the tattoo that inspired Jenna's amazing work.

Mirandi Riwoe, Laura Elvery, Melanie Saward, Lauren Mitchell, and Alexandra Patterson: for always being my cheerleaders, listening to my complaints, and sharing in my highs and lows. Shu-Ling Chua: one of my inspirations, I've always seen you as my writing 姊姊. I will always treasure your words and insights. Alice Pung: you've supported my writing from the very beginning. Thank you for your words of encouragement. Jessica Friedmann and Siang Lu: for reading previous versions of this book in its entirety and providing me with commentary even though you were under no obligation to do so.

The Katharine Susannah Prichard Writers' Centre and the Wheeler Centre's Hot Desk Fellowship program: for providing me with the space and quiet to write to my heart's content. Express Media – in particular, the Toolkits program, and Tom Doig, who ran the non-fiction course I participated in. The Queensland Literary Awards, Arts Queensland, and the Queensland Writers Centre: for assisting in the professional development I needed to get my manuscript over the line. A special thank you to Jenny Summerson and the Queensland Library Foundation, and the judges of the Glendower Award for an Emerging Queensland Writer in 2022: Madonna Duffy, Shastra Deo, George Haddad, and Amanda O'Callaghan.

Andrea, Dan, Lisa, Mandy, Marty, Ruby: your friendship means the world to me. Thank you for the chats, the laughs, the hugs, the food, and the encouragement.

Acknowledgements

Autumn, Summer, Spring: for the entertainment and the cuddles, for keeping me company during the days and nights when writing seemed like the most difficult thing in the world, and for teaching me that sometimes it's okay to rest (read: do nothing but sleep and eat all weekend). Summer – I will miss you so much, but part of you will live on through this book.

Yen-Chii: I love you so, so much. Thank you for your understanding and your quiet support.

Josh: for holding my hand during it all, listening to me talk about this book for years on end, filming my awkward acceptance speeches in the park, and giving me the space and time to write. Thank you, big duck. I love you.

I'd also like to acknowledge the Traditional Owners of the Lands on which this book was written: the Jagera and Turrbal Peoples, the Yugambeh People, the Awabakal and Worimi Peoples, the Bunurong Boon Wurrung and Wurundjeri Woi Wurrung Peoples of the Eastern Kulin Nation, and the Whadjuk Noongar People.

And finally, to the Brisbane writing community: thank you for being the kindest and most supportive bunch of legends a writer could ever ask for. I hope this never changes.

Variations or excerpts of the essays in this book have previously appeared in the following publications. Thank you to the editors of these publications – in particular, Ashley Hay, Caitlin Chang, and Candice Chung.

— 'Let's talk about sex – what I wish I knew as an Asian-Australian teen', *SBS Voices*, 1 June 2018.
— 'The Very Model of an Model Ethnic Minority', *Meanjin*, Summer 2018.
— 'The trauma of discipline', *Griffith Review*, Edition 65: *Crimes and Punishments*, 2019.
— 'I wish I could have talked to my mum in her own language about boys', *SBS Voices*, 21 February 2020.
— 'Yellow Fever', *Meanjin*, Autumn 2021.
— 'I want to see more racial diversity in the kink community', *SBS Pride*, 23 June 2022.

Further Texts

Me

1: Shame

Fecan, I. (Producer). (2016–2021). *Kim's Convenience* [Television series]. Toronto, Canada: Thunderbird Films.

Fung, H. (1999). Becoming a moral child: The socialization of shame among young Chinese children. *Ethos 27(2)*, 180–209. <www.jstor.org/stable/640656>.

2: Pleasure

Ah-King, M., Barron, A.B. & Herberstein, M.E. (2014). Genital evolution: Why are females still understudied? *PLoS Biology, 12(5)*. <doi.org/10.1371/journal.pbio.1001851>.

Barrica, A. (2018, January 18). How can we teach consent

if we don't teach about pleasure? *The Establishment.* <theestablishment.co/how-can-we-teach-consent-without-pleasure-91ec6e451585/>.

Brontë, C. (1847). *Jane Eyre.* London: Smith, Elder & Co.

Chalmers, J. & Jones, C. (2016, March 10). Why the clitoris doesn't get the attention it deserves – and why this matters. *The Conversation.* <theconversation.com/why-the-clitoris-doesnt-get-the-attention-it-deserves-and-why-this-matters-53157>.

Chua, S. (2020). *Echoes.* Australia: Somekind Press.

Desai, N. (Director). (2022). *The Principles of Pleasure* [Television series]. United States: Netflix.

Greenfield, R. (2013, January 8). A brief history of CES Booth Babes. *The Atlantic.* <www.theatlantic.com/technology/archive/2013/01/ces-booth-babes-history/319817/>.

Rhys, J. (1966). *Wide Sargasso Sea.* New York City, United States: W. W. Norton.

3: Kink

Graham, B.C., Butler, S.E., McGraw, R., Cannes, S.M. & Smith, J. (2016). Member perspectives on the role of BDSM communities. *The Journal of Sex Research, 53(8)*, 895–909. <http://doi.org/10.1080/00224499.2015.1067758>.

Martinez, K. (2016). Somebody's fetish: Self-objectification and body satisfaction among consensual sadomasochists. *The Journal of Sex Research, 53(1)*, 35–44.

Ostani, M. (2019, May 21). The 'good' and 'bad' feminist: Coming to terms with my kinks. *Archer Magazine.* <archermagazine.

com.au/2019/05/coming-to-terms-with-my-kinks/>.

Ratcliff-Elder, A., Pedersen, C.L., & Reichl, A.J. (2019). Whips & chains excite me: BDSM and social acceptance in the context of normative influences. *Kwantlen Psychology Student Journal*, *1*. <journals.kpu.ca/index.php/KPSJ/article/view/399>.

Her

4: Monsters

Chu, J.M. (Director). (2018). *Crazy Rich Asians* [Film]. United States & Singapore: SK Global.

Chua, A. (2011). *Battle Hymn of the Tiger Mother*. London, United Kingdom: Penguin Random House.

Poe, E.A. (1839). *The Fall of the House of Usher*. In *Burton's Gentleman's Magazine*.

Teo, S. (2018). *Ponti*. New York, United States: Simon & Schuster.

Yahp, B. (1992). *The Crocodile Fury*. Pymble, Australia: Angus & Robertson.

5: Language

Bergmann, C., Sprenger, S.A., & Schmid, M.S. (2015). The impact of language co-activation on L1 and L2 speech fluency. *Acta Psychologica*, *161*, 25–35. <doi.org/10.1016/j.actpsy.2015.07.015>.

Gallo, F., Bermudez-Margaretto, B., Shtyrov, Y., Abutalebi, J., Kreiner, H., Chitaya, T., Petrova, A. & Myachykov, A.

(2021). First language attrition: What it is, what it isn't, and what it can be. *Frontiers in Human Neuroscience, 15(686388)*, 1–20. <doi.org/10.3389/fnhum.2021.686388>.

Köpke, B. & Genevska-Hanke, D. (2018) First language attrition and dominance: Same same or different? *Frontiers in Psychology, 9(1963)*, 1–16. <doi.org/10.3389/fpsyg.2018.01963>.

Yu, Z., Chan, S., & Abdullah, A.N. (2013). Mandarin attrition among tertiary students, *Pertanika Journal of Social Science and Humanities, 21*, 217–34.

Zhang, D. (2010). Language maintenance and language shift among Chinese immigrant parents and their second-generation children in the US, *Bilingual Research Journal, 33(1)*, 42–60. <doi.org/10.1080/15235881003733258>.

Us

6: Yellow Fever

Chow, K. (2018, September 27). If we called ourselves yellow. *NPR.* <www.npr.org/sections/codeswitch/2018/09/27/647989652/if-we-called-ourselves-yellow>.

7: Race Traitor

Bader, S. (2017). Asian men as targets of sexual racism in the gay community. *American Cultural Studies Capstone Research Papers, 8*, 1–22. <cedar.wwu.edu/fairhaven_acscapstone/8>.

Eng, D.L. & Han, S. (2018). *Racial Melancholia, Racial Dissociation: On the social and psychic lives of Asian Americans.*

Durham: Duke University Press.

Nemoto, K. (2019). *Racing Romance: Love, power, and desire among Asian American/white couples*. New Brunswick: Rutgers University Press.

8: An Oriental Flower

Bishop, S. & Limmer, M. (2018). Negotiating the edge: The rationalization of sexual risk taking among western male sex tourists to Thailand. *The Journal of Sex Research, 55(7)*, 871–79. <doi.org/10.1080/00224499.2017.1365329>.

Brough, J., Chessell, B. & Miller, S. (Directors). (2016–2019). *The Family Law* [Television series]. Australia: Matchbox Pictures.

Chen, C. (Director). (2018). *Homecoming Queens* [Television series]. Australia: SBS.

Chen, C. (Director). (2021). *New Gold Mountain* [Television series]. Australia: Goalpost Television.

Fine, A. & Lee, S. (Executive producers). (2013–2019) *Agents of S.H.I.E.L.D* [Television series]. Los Angeles, United States: ABC Studios & Marvel Television.

Hamadi, L. (2014). Edward Said: The postcolonial theory and the literature of colonisation, *European Scientific Journal, 2*, 39–46.

Herath, T. (2016). Women and Orientalism: 19th century representations of the harem by European female travellers and Ottoman women, *Constellations, 7(1)*, 10. <doi.org/10.29173/cons27054>.

Kasdan, J., Khan, N. & Mar, M. (Executive producers).

(2015–2020). *Fresh off the Boat* [Television series]. Los Angeles, United States: Fierce Baby Productions.

Lee, M. (Writer) & Cáceres, L. (Director). *Going Down* [Theatre]. Sydney, Australia: Sydney Theatre Company.

Leitch, D. (Director). (2018). *Deadpool 2* [Film]. United States: 20th Century Fox.

Singer, B. (Director). (2014). *X-Men: Days of Future Past* [Film]. United States: Marvel Entertainment.

Wang, L. (Director). (2019). *The Farewell* [Film]. United States: Ray Productions.

Ward, T.J. & Lay, W.D. (2019). *Park Statue Politics: World War II comfort women memorials in the United States*. Bristol, United Kingdom: E-International Relations.

Notes

Me

2: Pleasure

1. Frederick, D.A., St John, H.K., Garcia, J.R. & Lloyd, E.A. (2018). Differences in orgasm frequency among gay, lesbian, bisexual, and heterosexual men and women in a US national sample. *Archives of Sexual Behavior*, *47*, 273–88. <doi.org/10.1007/s10508-017-0939-z>.
2. Liew, G.S. (2019). *Careen*. Virginia, United States: Noemi Press.
3. Nao, V.K. (2019, August 21). Careening: An interview with Grace Shuyi Liew. *Los Angeles Review of Books*. <lareviewofbooks.org/article/careening-an-interview-with-grace-shuyi-liew/>.
4. Richters, J., de Visser, R.O., Badcock, P.B., Smith, A.M.A., Rissel, C., Simpson, J.M. & Grulich, A. (2014). Masturbation, paying for sex, and other sexual activities: The Second Australian Study of Health and Relationships. *Sexual Health*, *11(5)*, 461–71.

5. Mosbergen, D. (2013, August 29). Cliteracy 101: Artist Sophia Wallace wants you to know the truth about the clitoris. *The Huffington Post.* <www.huffpost.com/entry/cliteracy_n_3823983?ri18n=true>.

6. Wallace, S. (2012). CLITERACY, 100 Natural Laws. *Sophia Wallace.* <www.sophiawallace.art/works#/cliteracy-100-natural-laws/>.

7. Wallace, S. (2013). ΑΔΑΜΑΣ. *Sophia Wallace.* <www.sophiawallace.art/works#/adamas/>.

8. Wallace, S. CLITERACY, 100 Natural Laws.

9. Posner, J. (Writer) & Laskowski, C. (Producer). (2018). The female orgasm. *Explained* [Television series]. Washington DC, United States: Vox Media.

10. Nolan, M. (2014, December 9). Guide to masturbating. *Oh Joy Sex Toy.* <www.ohjoysextoy.com/masturbate/>.

11. Desai, N. (Director) & Agha, S. (Producer). (2022). *The Principles of Pleasure* [Television series]. New York, United States: The Front.

12. Safronova, V. (2019, January 18). What's so 'indecent' about female pleasure? *The New York Times.* <www.nytimes.com/2019/01/18/style/sex-toy-ces.html>.

13. Safronova, V. What's so 'indecent' about female pleasure?

14. Mahdawi, A. (2013, January 12). Smart forks and booth babes at CES: The cutting edge of innovation. *The Guardian.* <www.theguardian.com/commentisfree/2013/jan/11/ces-smart-forks-booth-babes>.

15. Tokar, L. (2011, January 14). Tech promos @ CES-impersonators or booth babes? *The SSD Review.* <www.thessdreview.com/daily-news/latest-buzz/tech-promos-ces-impersonators-or-booth-babes/>.

16. HyperShop body-painted models at Las Vegas CES exhibit. (2013, January 26). *The Straits Times.* <www.straitstimes.com/singapore/hypershop-body-painted-models-at-las-vegas-ces-exhibit>.

17. Haddock, L. (2021, April 14). Open letter to CES. *Lora DiCarlo.* <loradicarlo.com/blog/open-letter-to-ces/>.

18. Safronova, V. What's so 'indecent' about female pleasure?

19. Lofgreen, A.M., Mattson, R.E., Wagner, S.A., Ortiz, E.G. & Johnson, M.D. (2021). Situational and dispositional determinants of college men's perception of women's sexual desire and consent to sex: A factorial vignette analysis. *Journal of Interpersonal Violence, 36(1–2)*. <doi.org/10.1177/0886260517738777>.

20. Lynch, A. (2021, March 12). Open letter regarding strategy for the prevention of violence against women and children. *Women's Legal Service Qld*. <wlsq.org.au/open-letter-regarding-strategy-for-the-prevention-of-violence-against-women-and-children/>.

21. Hills, P.J., Seib, E., Pleva, M., Smythe, J., Gosling, M. & Cole, T. (2020). Consent, wantedness, and pleasure: Three dimensions affecting the perceived stress of and judgements of rape in sexual encounters. *Journal of Experimental Psychology: Applied, 26(1)*, 171–97.

22. Hills, P.J., Seib, E., Pleva, M., Smythe, J., Gosling, M. & Cole, T. Consent, wantedness, and pleasure: Three dimensions affecting the perceived stress of and judgements of rape in sexual encounters.

23. Law, M. (Writer) & Christian, C. (Producer). (2017). *Single Asian Female* [Theatre]. Brisbane, Australia: La Boîte Theatre.

24. Nao, V.K. Careening: An interview with Grace Shuyi Liew.

25. Chua, Shu-Ling. (2016, June 16). Them spitting eels. *Peril Magazine*.

26. Pham, L. (2016). *Fantasian*. New York City, United States: Badlands Unlimited.

27. Pham, L. *Fantasian*.

28. Pham, L. *Fantasian*.

29. Pham, L. *Fantasian*.

3: Kink

1. Eells, J. (2011, April 14). Rihanna: Queen of pain. *Rolling Stone*. <www.rollingstone.com/music/music-news/rihanna-queen-of-pain-117943/>.

2. Eells, J. Rihanna: Queen of pain.

3. Ten Brink, S., Coppens, V., Huys, W. & Morrens, M. (2021). The

psychology of kink: A survey study into the relationships of trauma and attachment style with BDSM interests. *Sexuality Research & Social Policy, 18(1)*, 1–12. <doi.org/10.1007/s13178-020-00438-w>.

4. Russo, C. (2016). *Hojōjutsu: The warrior's art of the rope.* Turin, Italy: Yoshin Ryu Editions.

Her

4: Monsters

1. Lacan, J. (1949). *Écrits: A selection.* New York, United States: Taylor and Francis.

2. Živković, M. (2000). The double as the 'unseen' of culture: Toward a definition of doppelganger. *Linguistics and Literature, 2(7)*, 121–28.

3. Wang, W. (2017). *Chemistry: A novel.* New York City, United States: Knopf.

4. Lee, J. (2018). East Asian 'China Doll' or 'Dragon Lady'? *Bridges: An Undergraduate Journal of Contemporary Connections, 3*, 1. <scholars.wlu.ca/cgi/viewcontent.cgi?article=1026&context=bridges_contemporary_connections>.

5. Sweet, M. (2008, February 6). Snakes, slaves and seduction. *The Guardian.* <www.theguardian.com/film/2008/feb/06/china.world>.

6. Said, E. (1978). *Orientalism.* New York City, United States: Pantheon Books.

7. Ang, I. (2003). Together-in-difference: Beyond diaspora, into hybridity. *Asian Studies Review, 27(2)*, 141–54.

8. Tucker, S. (2000). Your worst nightmare: Hybridised demonology in Asian-Australian women's writing. *Journal of Australian Studies, 24(65)*, 150–57.

9. Lai, S. (2004). Sympathy for lady vengeance: Feminist ghosts and monstrous women of Asia. *The Lifted Brow, 23*, 18–22. <search.informit.org/doi/10.3316/informit.444648409740292>.

10. Paramaditha, I. (2018, September. 13). 'Ponti' is about

how society turns women into monsters. *Electric Literature.* <electricliterature.com/ponti-is-about-how-society-turns-women-into-monsters/>.

5: Language

1. Poplack, S. (2001). Code switching: Linguistic. *International Encyclopaedia of the Social & Behavioural Sciences*, 2062.
2. Wang, W. *Chemistry: A novel.*
3. Schmid, M., & Köpke, B. (2017). The relevance of first language attrition to theories of bilingual development. *Linguistic Approaches to Bilingualism, 7(6)*, 637–67.
4. Schmid, M. (2018, March 29). Expats beware: Losing confidence in your mother tongue could cost you a job. *The Conversation.* <theconversation.com/expats-beware-losing-confidence-in-your-mother-tongue-could-cost-you-a-job-92243>.
5. Lo Bianco, J. (2009). Second languages and Australian schooling. *Australian Council for Educational Research.* <research.acer.edu.au/cgi/viewcontent.cgi?article=1007&context=aer>.
6. Lo Bianco, J. Second languages and Australian schooling.
7. Guo, X. (2007). *A concise Chinese-English dictionary for lovers.* Translated by Talese, N.A. New York, United States: Doubleday.
8. Guo, X. *A concise Chinese-English dictionary for lovers.*
9. Tudge, A. (2018, March 7). The integration challenge: Maintaining successful Australian multiculturalism. *Alan Tudge.* <www.alantudge.com.au/speeches/the-integration-challenge-maintaining-successful-australian-multiculturalism/>.
10. Morrison, S. (2020, September 17). Big changes to citizenship test puts emphasis on Australian values. *9News.* <www.9news.com.au/national/australian-citizenship-test-upgraded-focus-on-national-values/2526d303-24cc-4f53-9d65-b3f8bc987e8e>.
11. Yahp, B. (1988). Kuala Lumpur story. In S. Gunew & J. Mahyuddin (Eds.), *Beyond the Echo: Multicultural women's writing*, 236–42. Brisbane, Australia: University of Queensland Press.

Us

6: Yellow Fever

1. Keevak, M. (2011). *Becoming Yellow: A short history of racial thinking.* New Jersey, United States: Princeton University Press.
2. Keevak, M. *Becoming Yellow: A short history of racial thinking.*
3. Keevak, M. *Becoming Yellow: A short history of racial thinking.*
4. Yellow Fever. (2019, May 7). *World Health Organization.* <www.who.int/news-room/fact-sheets/detail/yellow-fever>.
5. Triple J Hack. (2017, February 14). Racial dating: Why you swipe right for some and not others. *ABC.* <www.abc.net.au/triplej/programs/hack/are-you-a-racist-dater/8269564>.
6. Hundreds, B. (2014, May 20). Porn in the USA: My interview with Asa Akira. *The Hundreds.* <thehundreds.com/blogs/bobby-hundreds/asa_akira>.
7. Hundreds, B. Porn in the USA: My interview with Asa Akira.
8. Zhang, J. (2017, January 31). The other 'Yellow Fever' – Why are some people exclusively attracted to Asian women? *VICE.* <www.vice.com/en/article/xyvyxn/the-other-yellow-fever-why-are-some-men-exclusively-attracted-to-asian-women>.
9. McGowan, K. (2017, July 19). Me So Hungry to change name after online backlash. *The Des Moines Register.*
10. Kubrick, S. (Director & Producer). (1987). *Full Metal Jacket* [Film]. United States: Warner Bros. Pictures.
11. Brunback, K. (2021, August 2). Man pleads guilty to 4 Asian spa killings, sentenced to life without parole. *PBS News Hour.* <www.pbs.org/newshour/nation/georgia-man-pleading-guilty-to-4-of-8-asian-spa-killings>.
12. Zheng, R. (2016). Why yellow fever isn't flattering: A case against racial fetishes. *Journal of the American Philosophical Association, 2(3)*, 400–19. <doi.org/10.1017/apa.2016.25>.
13. Dr Stephen Kershnar. *Fredonia State University of New York.* <www.fredonia.edu/academics/colleges-schools/college-liberal-arts-

sciences/philosophy/faculty/Stephen-Kershnar>.

14. Kershnar, S. (2019). In defense of Asian romantic preference. *International Journal of Applied Philosophy, 32(2)*, 243–56.

15. Kershnar, S. In defense of Asian romantic preference.

16. Hall, L. (2008). How to be Japanese. In A. Pung (Ed.), *Growing Up Asian in Australia*, 227–34. Melbourne, Australia: Black Inc.

17. Hall, L. How to be Japanese. In A. Pung (Ed.), *Growing Up Asian in Australia*.

18. Prasso, S. About. (2023). <sheridanprasso.com/about>.

19. Yoon, C. (2005). Sheridan Prasso: Seeing past the stereotypes. *Asia Society.* <asiasociety.org/sheridan-prasso-seeing-past-stereotypes>.

20. What is anthropology? *UC Davis.* <anthropology.ucdavis.edu/undergraduate/what-is-anthropology>.

21. Saw, Y. (2020, July 20) Half-Asians face hyper pressure to be beautiful. *SBS.* <www.sbs.com.au/guide/article/2020/07/27/half-asians-face-hyper-pressure-be-beautiful>.

22. Hu, N. (2023, January 23). Dispelling the myth that Asian vaginas are tighter. *Healthline.* <www.healthline.com/health/womens-health/tight-vagina-asian-stereotype#But-a-dying-myth-doesnt-mean-the-effects-disappear-along-with-it->.

23. I was taught to be proud of my tight Asian p*ssy – Here's why I wish I hadn't been. (2016, July 20). *Everyday Feminism.* <everydayfeminism.com/2016/07/be-proud-tight-asian-pssy/>.

24. Khmelnitski, N. (2023, January 24). A Chinese woman taking naked photos of men in the UK. *WÜL Magazine.* <www.wulmagazine.com/photography/yushi-li>.

25. Jansen, C. (2021, February 9). Why this Chinese photographer takes pictures of naked Western men. *Elephant Magazine.* <elephant.art/why-this-chinese-photographer-takes-pictures-of-naked-western-men/>.

26. Jansen, C. Why this Chinese photographer takes pictures of naked Western men.

7: Race Traitor

1. Ng, N. (2017, July 10). Asian men endure a unique type of racism (and why Asian women shouldn't ignore it). *NextShark*. <nextshark.com/asian-men-endure-unique-type-racism-asian-women-shouldnt-ignore>.

2. Romero, E. (2017, April 12). Dear Asian women, I'm calling you out on this one. *NextShark*. <nextshark.com/dear-asian-women-im-calling-one-aesthetic-distance>.

3. Chavez, A. (2017, April 17). On interracial dating, toxic masculinity, and feminist agency. *Medium*. <medium.com/@austintexaschav/on-interracial-dating-toxic-asian-masculinity-and-feminist-agency-a7289219323a>.

4. Bhabha, H. (1984). Of mimicry and man: The ambivalence of colonial discourse. *October, 28*, 125–33.

5. Bhabha, H. Of mimicry and man.

6. Cheng, A.A. (2001). *The Melancholy of Race: Psychoanalysis, assimilation, and hidden grief.* Oxford, United Kingdom: Oxford University Press. Reproduced with permission of the Licensor through PLSclear.

7. Cheng, A.A. *The Melancholy of Race: Psychoanalysis, assimilation, and hidden grief.*

8. Ahmed, T. (2015, February 9). Men forgotten in violence debate. *The Australian*.

9. Cheng, A.A. *The Melancholy of Race: Psychoanalysis, assimilation, and hidden grief.*

10. Robnett, B. & Feliciano, C. (2011). Patterns of racial-ethnic exclusion by internet daters. *Social Forces, 89(3)*, 807–28. <doi.org/10.1353/sof.2011.0008>.

11. Kao, G., Balistreri, K.S., Joyner, K. (2018). Asian American men in romantic dating markets. *Contexts, 17(4)*, 48–53. <doi.org/10.1177/1536504218812869>.

12. *What the Flip?* Grindr. <www.facebook.com/watch/?v=10155040306128237>.

13. McInerney, N. (Director) & Elkin-Jones, N. (Producer). (2017). *Date My Race* [Television series]. Sydney, Australia: Matchbox Pictures.

14. Ooi, J. (2021, November 25). On the emasculation of Asian men. *Shoes Off: Stories about Asian Australian culture* [Podcast]. <www.shoesoff.net/episodes/emasculation-asian-men>.

15. Chu, M. (2021, April 28). I was missing out when I refused to date Asian men. *SBS Voices*. <www.sbs.com.au/topics/voices/relationships/article/2021/04/28/i-was-missing-out-when-i-refused-date-asian-men>.

16. Ooi, J. On the emasculation of Asian men.

8: An Oriental Flower

1. Said, E. *Orientalism*.

2. Said, E. *Orientalism*.

3. Said, E. *Orientalism*.

4. Lang, C. (2020, June 26). The Asian American response to Black Lives Matter is part of a long, complicated history. *TIME*. <time.com/5851792/asian-americans-black-solidarity-history/>.

5. O'Donnell, J. (2022). Mapping social cohesion. *Scanlon Foundation Research Institute*. <scanloninstitute.org.au/sites/default/files/2022-11/MSC%202022_Report.pdf>.

6. Kassam, N. & Hsu, J. (2021). Being Chinese in Australia: Public opinion in Chinese communities. *The Lowy Institute*. <interactives.lowyinstitute.org/features/chinese-communities/reports/2021%20Being%20Chinese%20in%20Australia%20Poll%20–%20Lowy%20Institute.pdf>.

7. Liu, H. (2017). Beneath the white gaze: Strategic self-Orientalism among Chinese Australians. *Human Relations, 70(7)*, 781–804. <doi.org/10.1177/0018726716676323>.

8. Liu, H. Beneath the white gaze: Strategic self-Orientalism among Chinese Australians.

9. Liu, H. Beneath the white gaze: Strategic self-Orientalism among Chinese Australians.

10. Said, E. *Orientalism.*

11. Woan, S. (2008). White sexual imperialism: A theory of Asian feminist jurisprudence. *Washington and Lee Journal of Civil Rights and Justice, 14(2)*, 275–301.

12. Woan, S. White sexual imperialism: A theory of Asian feminist jurisprudence.

13. Ward, T.J. & Lay, W.D. (2019). *Park Statue Politics: World War II comfort women memorials in the United States.* Bristol, United Kingdom: E-International Relations.

14. Park, J. (2014, July 13). Former Korean 'comfort women' for US troops sue own government. *Reuters.* <www.reuters.com/article/uk-southkorea-usa-military-idINKBN0FI06O20140713>.

15. Rivers, T. (1990, October). Oriental girls. *Gentleman's Quarterly* (British ed.).

16. Woan, S. White sexual imperialism: A theory of Asian feminist jurisprudence.

17. Said, E. *Orientalism.*

18. Akita, K. (2006). Orientalism and the binary of fact and fiction in *Memoirs of a Geisha. Global Media Journal, 5(9)*, 1–11.

19. Akita, K. Orientalism and the binary of fact and fiction in *Memoirs of a Geisha.*

20. Green, J. (2017, March 23). Theater review: Why are we in *Miss Saigon? Vulture.* <www.vulture.com/2017/03/theater-review-why-are-we-in-miss-saigon.html>.

21. Phi, T.T. (2009). Game over: Asian Americans and video game representation. *Transformative Works and Cultures, 2.* <doi.org/10.3983/twc.2009.084>.

22. Ishii, S. (2014). 'Unless she had implants, she must be Chinese': A feminist analysis of players' responses to representations of Chinese and Japanese female video game characters. *Loading … The Journal of the Canadian Game Studies Association, 8(13)*, 81–99. <loading.gamestudies.ca>.

23. Phi, T.T. Game over: Asian Americans and video game representation.

24. Marsha, A. (2018, January 9). What's the deal with men's rights activists and Asian fetishes? *Vice.* <www.vice.com/en/article/9kqqn3/whats-the-deal-with-mens-rights-activists-and-asian-fetishes>.

25. Cho, S. (1997). Converging stereotypes in racialized sexual harassment: Where the model minority meets Suzie Wong. In A. Wing (Ed.), *Critical Race Feminism.* New York, United States: New York University Press.

26. Rivers, T. Oriental girls.